PORTLAND HEAD LIGHT
THE GRAND DADDY OF ALL LIGHTHOUSES

By Timothy E. Harrison

Published and copyrighted by
FogHorn Publishing, Inc.
P.O. Box 68, Wells, Maine 04090
207-646-7000

Designed by BOMA, LLC

Printed in the United States of America
First Printing 2006

TABLE OF
CONTENTS

INTRODUCTION

Portland Head Light:
The Grand Daddy of All Lighthouses

Without question, Portland Head Light is one of the most recognizable and visited lighthouses in the United States, if not the world.

With its spectacular setting, no other lighthouse symbolizes the coast of Maine, or is more associated with Maine, than Portland Head Light at Fort Williams Park in Cape Elizabeth, Maine.

Portland Head Light is one of the most historic structures in the United States of America. In fact, one can learn more about the early history of the United States of America by studying the history of Portland Head Light than any other historic structure in the nation.

It would be fair to guess the image of Portland Head Light has been used by more firms to promote their products and services than any other structure.

Portland Head Light has appeared on countless calendars.

There is not a day that goes by, no matter how severe the weather, that one can visit Portland Head Light and find others doing the same.

Portland Head Light is magical, majestic and mysterious.

Portland Head Light is everything that most people, when seeing it for the first time, imagine a lighthouse should look like.

Portland Head Light represents many different things to many different people. To some, it represents strength, to others it represents solace, to some it represents romance and to others, beauty.

Portland Head Light truly is the "Grand Daddy" of all American lighthouses.

PORTLAND HEAD LIGHT
THE GRAND DADDY OF ALL LIGHTHOUSES

A Pictorial Journey Through Time

By Timothy E. Harrison

It has often been said that "lighthouses are to America what castles are to Europe." This statement may be somewhat far-fetched but it does make its point. In reality, lighthouses are among the oldest standing historic buildings in America, and some of them date back to colonial days before we were a nation.

This book is not meant to be an in-depth study of Portland Head Light. It is instead a "Pictorial Journey Through Time" history book that will give you a greater understanding and appreciation of one of the most famous lighthouses in the world.

Through the pages of this book, you will be able to learn through historic photographs, with informative text, the story of this famous lighthouse from its early beginnings through its evolution to what it is today — a memorial to our nation's maritime ancestors who helped make this nation the great country that it is today.

DEDICATION

This book is dedicated to the memory
of the lighthouse keepers and their family members of the
United States Lighthouse Service and the United States Coast
Guard who dedicated their lives to keeping the lights burning for
the safe passage of life and commerce that led to the rapid growth
of our nation as a world leader.

Proceeds of this book go to support the efforts
of the nonprofit American Lighthouse Foundation
to help their efforts to save and preserve our nation's lighthouses
and the history and artifacts associated with them.

www.LighthouseFoundation.org

IN APPRECIATION

There are many people to thank for helping make this book possible. But none would be more important than Ken Black, my longtime friend and mentor, who many years ago got me involved in the lighthouse preservation movement. Ken Black, who is the founder of the Maine Lighthouse Museum, is known in lighthouse circles as "Mr. Lighthouse" because he is credited with being one of the leaders in the early years of lighthouse preservation long before most people realized that we were at an era when our lighthouse history was on the verge of being lost forever.

Special thanks go to Donna Strout, a descendant of the Strout family of dedicated lighthouse keepers who for so many years tended the lighthouse at Portland Head Light. It was her late father, John Strout, who introduced me many years ago to his strong conviction of keeping alive the history of Portland Head Light. It was then Donna's continuation of that dedication that helped move the project forward as she searched through old family records to help uncover bits of history that might otherwise have been forgotten.

A debt of gratitude is owed to John Sterling, the grandson of Portland Head Light's last civilian keeper, Robert T. Sterling, who supplied me with a tremendous wealth of information and historic photographs that helped put the finishing touches to the book.

It was the dedication of Kathleen Finnegan that helped immensely by doing all the scanning of photographs and supervising the layout and design of this book — work that she did after her real job's workday was over.

In no special order, other special thanks go to the following who in one way or another over the years helped supply historical information, research material, research time and photographs that were used for this book. They are: Wayne Brooking, the Cape Elizabeth Historical Society, Earle Shettleworth, Jr., Maine Historic Preservation Commission, Robert Trapani, Jr., Judi Kearney, Dee Leveille, *Lighthouse Digest* magazine, James W. Claflin, Jeff Shook, Lorraine Morong, Shirley Morong, Jeanne Gross, Museum at Portland Head Light, William O. Thomson, Jeremy D'Entremont, J. Candace Clifford, Steve Frank, Dave Gamage, South Portland Historical Society, Rusty Nelson, Geraldine Reed, Tom Reed, Edward Ellis, Dorothy Black, Boma LCC, Elaine Amass Ellis, *Downeast Magazine*, Portland Public Library, Richard Clayton, Bob and Sandra Shanklin — "The Lighthouse People," Ted Panayotoff, Lou Marc-Aurele, Gerry Braun, National Archives, the Library of Congress, the United States Coast Guard, and the many lighthouse aficionados, who over the years have done so much to help save and preserve our nation's lighthouse history and heritage. I'm sure there are others to thank and I apologize to anyone that I might have forgotten.

And last but not least, thanks to my mother, Dorothy Harrison, my biggest fan.

CHAPTER 1

THE BEGINNING

In the 1700s, Maine was a territory of the Commonwealth of Massachusetts and the city of Portland was known as Falmouth. In 1787, Portland and Falmouth split into two separate towns.

By the late 1700s, Portland Harbor had become one of America's busiest seaports. The local merchants petitioned John Hancock, the governor of Massachusetts, requesting that a lighthouse be built at Portland Head, in the community of Cape Elizabeth. Under Hancock's orders, construction of the lighthouse began.

With the ratification of the United States Constitution in June of 1788, the new federal government of the United States came into being. On August 7, 1789, the First Congress of the United States passed its first Public Works Act when it federalized all lighthouses in the United States. The lighthouses were placed under the control of the Treasury Department and Alexander Hamilton, its first Secretary. The new federal government came up with the necessary funds to complete construction, and the lighthouse at Portland Head was completed in 1791.

The original plans called for the lighthouse to be a stone tower, 58 feet tall. However, when it was realized that the lighthouse could not be seen from the south, it was decided to make the tower 72 feet high.

Although Alexander Hamilton was technically in charge of all the lighthouses for many years, the lighthouse keepers were personally appointed by the President of the United States, generally as a reward for services performed. In this case, President George Washington appointed Revolutionary War veteran Joseph Greenleaf as the first lighthouse keeper. Unfortunately for Greenleaf, the new government did not appropriate any money to pay him, but in exchange for his duties, he was allowed to live in the keeper's house for free. By 1793, Congress approved a salary for Greenleaf of $160.00 per year.

John Hancock, a signer of the Declaration of Independence, approved the construction of Portland Head Light when he was governor of the Commonwealth of Massachusetts.

A Revolutionary War veteran, Alexander Hamilton, became the first Secretary of the Treasury and the first person to be in charge of United States lighthouses. On July 11, 1804, at the age of 47, in a duel with Aaron Burr, Hamilton was mortally wounded.

George Washington, the first President of the United States, personally appointed the first lighthouse keeper of Portland Head Light.

CHAPTER 2

A CHANGE IN HEIGHT

The original plans called for the tower of Portland Head Light to be 58 feet tall, however, this was changed during construction to 72 feet tall.

Ever since it was built, there had been constant discussion about what the proper height of the tower should be for vessels to be able to see the beacon.

In 1813 the tower was lowered by 20 feet.

In 1864 it was raised by 20 feet.

In 1883 the tower was shortened by 20 feet. Also, at that time, a less powerful fourth order lens replaced its powerful second order lens.

After numerous complaints about the shorter tower with the weaker lens, in 1884 the tower was raised by 20 feet and a second order lens was again installed in the lantern room and was lit on January 15, 1885.

This sketch, dated October 7, 1882, was sent to the Lighthouse Board in Washington for approval showing how the tower at Portland Head appeared with a new lantern room and weaker lens before it was lowered by 20 feet.

Portland Head Light with its original keeper's house and when the tower was 20 feet shorter than it is now. The keeper's house shown here was eventually torn down and replaced. The structure in front of the lighthouse was the fogbell tower in use at the time.

The year of this photograph is unknown. As well as showing the tower at its taller height, it shows an amazing amount of construction at the lighthouse, which is believed to be the building of the new keeper's house. On the back of the photo is written, "To my real friend - Mickey. The most dearly of all, Capt. Strout (lighthouse keeper)."

From Portland Head Light, on a clear day, generally in the late afternoon, when looking way out into Casco Bay, you will see the gleaming white tower of Halfway Rock Lighthouse. Like Ram Island Ledge Light, which sits in the water a short distance from Portland Head Light, Casco Bay's Halfway Rock Lighthouse sits exposed to all the fury that Mother Nature can throw at it. The last keepers were removed from the lighthouse in 1975 and the tower was automated. It is now licensed to the American Lighthouse Foundation. When Halfway Rock Lighthouse was built in 1871, it was decided that Portland Head Light had become less important and should be lowered by 20 feet, a plan that did not happen until 1883. However, there were so many complaints that the tower at Portland Head was raised back to its original height.

CHAPTER 3

DRESSING UP

Prior to 1893, lighthouse keepers used their own ideas as to what they would wear, and since there were no specific regulations, they were largely free to dress as they pleased.

However, by 1893, there were specific regulations and manuals put into place that instructed them in the wearing of an official uniform.

Although the regulations and uniform design in the manuals changed slightly over the years, some of the keepers only loosely followed the manuals, while others followed the regulation to the rule. Apparently, some of the Lighthouse Service inspectors were more lenient than others. The uniform was designated to be navy blue with different weights and materials for the season. Eventually, a white hat and white uniform were permitted for summer months, but very few keepers actually had a white uniform.

The rules required that the keeper must always be in his dress uniform when the lighthouse grounds were open to the public. In locations such as Portland Head Light, where visitors always seem to be present, the keeper was often in uniform. However, at many of the remote locations, some keepers rarely wore their uniforms, but almost always wore the hat. However, when they would spot a lighthouse tender approaching, they knew the Lighthouse Inspector might be on board and they would hurriedly change into their uniform.

When the Lighthouse Service was merged into the Coast Guard in 1939, the lighthouse keepers were given the option to stay on as civilian keepers or join the Coast Guard. They split almost evenly in their choice. Generally, most of the civilian keepers continued to wear the old uniform. For a period of time, Coast Guard keepers also wore a lighthouse emblem of one style or another on their hats.

Many lighthouse locations had women lighthouse keepers, but interestingly, women were not required to wear any type of uniform and were allowed to dress as they pleased.

Brass buttons like these were worn on all uniforms of most employees of the U.S. Lighthouse Service, including lighthouse keepers, vessel officers and others of importance.

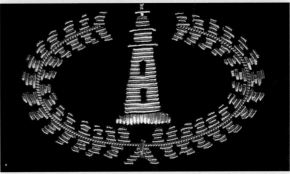

This style, or a very similar design, was the official emblem affixed on all hats worn by lighthouse keepers, engineers and captains of vessels of the United States Lighthouse Service until it was dissolved in 1939 and merged into the Coast Guard. However, the emblem continued to be used by civilian keepers until there were none left. However, some Coast Guard keepers continued to use the emblem on their hats as late as the 1950s.

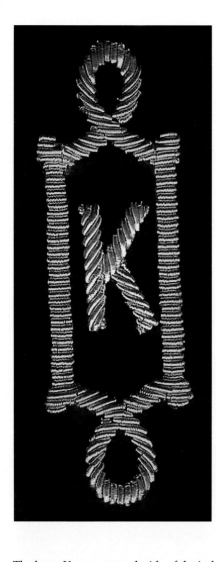 

Lighthouse keepers were awarded the red Efficiency Star for being commended by the Lighthouse Inspector at their quarterly inspections and were allowed to wear this star on their uniforms. If a keeper was awarded a red Efficiency Star for three years in a row, he was then given the Lighthouse Service Commissioner's blue Efficiency Star.

The letter K sewn on each side of the jacket lapel of a uniform indicated that the person was the head keeper at a lighthouse. The number 1 would mean 1st Assistant Keeper, the number 2 would mean 2nd Assistant Keeper and so forth. The letter E would mean lighthouse engineer. By the 1920s, gold service bars were introduced to be worn on the left sleeve near the cuff indicating the length of service. Each bar represented five years of service up to 20 years. A gold embroidered star was used for 25 years of service.

CHAPTER 4

A STROUT TRADITON

hen Joshua Freeman Strout became keeper of Portland Head Light in 1869, he started a family tradition of lighthouse keeping that would last until the mid-1900s.

As a young man of 18, Joshua F. Strout began his seagoing career as a ship's cook. In 1854, he took command of his own vessel. As his grandson John wrote about him in *Lighthouse Digest*, "He was one of those daring skippers who crowned sail on the tall barques, brigantines and full riggers that for five decades, in the middle of the last century, brought to our foreign trade a greatness and glory that remains unsurpassed in the history of the mercantile marine."

After an accidental fall onboard ship, he was forced to find a new career. Apparently his years of hardwork, knowledge of the sea, and contacts paid off when he received the appointment as keeper at Portland Head Light at a salary of $620 per year. Joshua Strout must have been a good negotiator since he was also able to secure his wife Mary the position of assistant keeper with a salary of $480 per annum.

Joshua Freeman Strout was no stranger to Portland Head when he accepted the position of keeper in 1869. His mother had been a housekeeper for Joshua Freeman, who was the fourth person to serve as the keeper of Portland Head Light, serving from 1820 to 1840. In fact, Strout's mother had such great respect for Joshua Freeman that she named her son after him. Little could she have dreamed at the time that the son she named after the lighthouse keeper would grow up to fill that job in 1869.

In those days, lard oil fueled the light and keep it lit. As recounted in an interview by May Whiting of the *Dearborn Independent* magazine with his son, Joseph, in 1925, he recounted how every day about four o'clock in the afternoon Joshua would say, "Time to get some fat, boys," and they would go down in the cellar, scoop up a bucketful and put it on the stove to warm. When it was so hot that they were barely able to handle it they would take it

Joshua Strout (1827-1907), keeper at Portland Head Light from 1869 to 1904.

up the tower and fill the lamp, then build a fire in the watch room to keep it from congealing.

Someone had to watch all night, for the fire had to be tended and the machinery wound every three hours to keep the oil flowing about the wicks. And many times it was the son's job to spend the night in the lantern room. The story went on to say that "those were weary hours for the lad, hours of loneliness and weirdness, which even a lifetime's acquaintance with the sea cannot dispel, nights with the surf running and the shimmering moonlight, or, in the dark of the moon, the dim starlight, and the unseen beating of the waves, restless as if with the memory of souls they have engulfed."

Joseph W. Strout was appointed assistant keeper at Portland Head Light in 1877. In 1904 he assumed the position of head keeper from his father Joshua, a position he held until 1928. He became one of the best known and best loved lighthouse keepers in history. Thousands of visitors visited the lighthouse every year to chat with "Capt'n Joe," as he affectionately became known. He is shown here posing with a birdhouse replica of the lighthouse that he built and put on the roof of the keeper's house at Portland Head.

After a long day's work, lighthouse keeper Joseph Strout takes a moment to relax for this 1924 photograph. If you look closely you will see his wife Mary in the window behind him and clothes drying on the line at the right side of the photograph.

Over 100 Years of Strout Service at Portland Head Light

Capt. Joshua Freeman Strout served at Portland Head Light from 1869 to 1904. His wife Mary served as his assistant for ten of those years. His son Joseph W. Strout became the assistant keeper in 1877 and served in that position until 1904 when he became the Head Keeper, a position he held until his retirement in 1928. Adding the few years that John A Strout served as Assistant Keeper, the Strout family dedicated nearly 90 years of their lives in service at Portland Head Light. Interestingly, if you were to add in the time that Joshua Freeman Strout's mother worked as a housekeeper at Portland Head Light for a previous keeper, the Strout family would have over 100 years of service at Portland Head Light.

Not including Joshua's mother's tenure as a housekeeper, if you add the years that John A Strout served at other New England lighthouses and at the Lighthouse Depot, the Strout family dedicated 128 years serving their country in the employment of the United States Lighthouse Service.

As well as being associated with Portland Head Light and Spring Point Ledge Light, the Strout name was also associated with other Maine lighthouses. Len Strout was the keeper at Portland Breakwater Lighthouse from 1866 to 1867 and Arthur Strout was an assistant keeper at Halfway Rock Lighthouse from 1929 to 1934.

Although the Strout family had, by far, the longest family tradition of lighthouse keeping at Portland Head Light, there was a previous father and son who also maintained the light at Portland Head. Barzillai Delano served as keeper of Portland Head Light from 1796 to 1820 and his son James was keeper from 1854 to 1861.

Lighthouse keeper Capt. Joseph Strout at the top of Portland Head Light in 1925. In the May 1997 issue of *Lighthouse Digest*, his grandson John wrote: *"There being no regulations in those days, he climbed the tower stairs over and over again to explain its wonders and to give visitors unrivaled and unbroken views of the sea from the lighthouse deck 101 feet above the water. However, regulations did require he wear the uniform at all hours while visitors were present. He was known to thousands of summer visitors. Each Christmas he received hundreds of remembrances such as fruit from California, candy, delicacies and gifts for the family from folks who had visited Portland Head Light and received his courtesies."*

Well-liked and popular, Capt. Joseph Strout was the most widely know of all Maine's lighthouse keepers. Notice the official emblem of the United States Lighthouse Service on his hat.

Lighthouse keeper Capt. Joseph Strout was proud of his flower garden at Portland Head Light. Today the beautiful flower gardens at Portland Head Light are maintained by volunteers.

Lighthouse keeper John A. Strout, shown in his uniform, was a third generation keeper at Portland Head Light.

John Strout shown here in the lantern room at Portland Head during a return visit after his retirement.

John A. Strout was born in the keeper's house at Portland Head Light on January 14, 1891. Like his father, grandfather and grandmother before him, he carried on the family tradition when at the age of 21 he became assistant keeper at Portland Head Light in 1912. As a boy at Portland Head Light he saw the Great White Fleet and the ships that in somber array fought in the Spanish-American War. He later recounted to his son seeing the magnificent full-rigged ships and even the six-masted schooners. He knew the names of their masters and met most of the crews when off-duty. As well as the battleships and other fighting vessels, he also knew the palatial yachts of the nation's millionaires.

Although the government broke the Strout family tradition when they transferred him to Graves Lighthouse in Massachusetts, where he served as assistant keeper for two years, John A. Strout continued with an amazing and illustrious career that his father and grandfather would have been proud of. He was then transferred again, this time to Bakers Island Lighthouse, also in Massachusetts where he served for two years. Apparently he wanted to return to Maine and he resigned from the Lighthouse Service to accept a job with the Burrows Screen Company in Portland, where he remained for three years. However, lighthouses were in his blood and he rejoined the Lighthouse Service to accept a position as Second Assistant Keeper at Boston Light where he served from 1921 to 1923.

He was then promoted to Assistant Keeper and sent to Great Point Lighthouse in Nantucket for two years. From there he went to the Gurnet Lighthouse in Plymouth, Massachusetts for another two years. Then he went on to serve for the next six years at Dumpling Rock Lighthouse, also in Massachusetts. Finally he got to return to Maine to serve near Portland Head at the Spring Point Ledge Lighthouse for one year, but left due to illness in 1931. He then accepted a shore position at the U.S. Lighthouse Service Buoy Depot at Little Diamond Island in Portland Harbor. He later finished his lighthouse career at the old buoy yard in Chelsea, Massachusetts. He recalled with fondness his days at Chelsea, recalling when a new crewman from a lightship was sent to shore to the Depot with orders to get a "bucket of steam" or a "left-handed wrench."

The Strout family kept the light during the "Great Age of Sail."

Photograph of a pen and ink drawing by an unknown artist that was presented to Joshua F. Strout, the head keeper at Portland Head Light from 1869 to 1904. This image shows the old keeper's house before it was torn down and replaced by the current structure that stands today.

CHAPTER 5

TIDAL WAVE

PORTLAND HEAD LIGHT ABSORBS A "MONSTER" 60-FOOT TIDAL WAVE, SAVES CITY FROM DESTRUCTION

Since 1791, through storm, fog and still, the guiding white beam of Portland Head Lighthouse has faithfully performed its duty to warn and protect seafarers entering the state of Maine's largest port at Portland Harbor. The beacon's rich lifesaving legacy, though renowned and respected by ship captains and crews the world over, seems to have done what few, if any, other sentinels of the coast can lay claim to. For on the terrifying night of December 28, 1887, at the height of a winter gale gone mad, this stoic sentinel not only safeguarded ships being battered about by the storm-tossed waters of Casco Bay. It also appears to have saved the entire port of the city of Portland from destruction.

At the time of the storm, no one in and around Portland Harbor had reason to be overly concerned. December gales in Casco Bay were hardly unusual events for mariners and lightkeepers at stations like Portland Head. During such severe storms, the keepers would often work together — forgoing much-needed rest to assist each other in keeping the light shining and fog signal sounding throughout the anxious ordeal. Yet, on this particular night, a moment of smashing horror would soon forever be etched in the minds of the lightkeeping Strout family.

The gale, which began around half-past nine in the evening, packed an intense punch that kept the lightkeepers extremely attentive to the station's equipment throughout the night. In addition, the men also took turns ensuring that a watchful eye was affixed on the seething seascape for possible ships in distress. As for the weather conditions, the December 31, 1887

edition of the *Decatur Daily Republican* newspaper records that the gale struck "at a time when, in this harbor, the wind seemed to be dying out. Up to that time, while the wind had been terrific, blowing 50 miles an hour, the rain falling continuously, Keeper Strout and his assistants, Joe and Gil Strout, had no idea that anything unusual was about to occur."

As the intensity of the storm built, so too did the keeper's anxieties. The stone tower's stout construction did not prevent the lighthouse from shaking in the face of the harrowing wind, nor did the structure absorb the shock of crushing waves against the rocky ledge below without exacting a heavy toll on the tattered nerves of the keepers and their families. Yet the worst was still to come.

Assistant Keeper Gil Strout recounts the moments prior to witnessing the unthinkable, saying in the *Decatur Daily Republican* account that "it was very clear, and we could see a long way out through the rain, and when the great wave made its appearance, we could see its whitecap way out and could watch its approach." The "great wave" that Assistant Keeper Strout referred to was a no ordinary wall of water riding the shoulders of an icy winter gale. In fact, King Neptune had never spawned a greater horror from the depths of the deep in this region, prior to the rogue wall of water taking direct aim on Portland Harbor.

Some news reporters called it a "tidal wave", while others described this volume of terrifying fright as a "monster wave." Regardless of the choice of description, everyone agreed with Maryland's *Frederick News* when it stated, "The volume of water was the largest ever observed at that point." Yet the sea-borne drama associated with the monster wave did not stop there. Nevada's *Reno Evening Gazette* cited the fact that, "The lightkeeper at Portland Head reports that this city had a narrow escape from destruction by a tidal wave during Wednesday night's storm."

But just what was this petrifying wave that threatened to bring calamities unknown down on unsuspecting Portland Harbor? The *Decatur Daily Republican* answers this question by saying, "Apparently, the monster wave came in the shape of a pyramid." Yet, despite the terror that they were witnessing right before their eyes, keepers Joshua, Joseph and Gil Strout had no doubt about the wave's unprecedented size and reach. The men reported the fact that the monster wave first collided with the outer line of the rock, and yet despite meeting the immovable resistance of the ledge, the "mass of water towered up even with the lighthouse itself," said the keepers.

In one spot near Portland Head Lighthouse, the rocky ledge forms a hardened line of etched mass that extends for approximately 100 feet along the sea line of Casco Bay and the shore. Within this rugged location is an opening nearly 40 feet deep and approximately 20 feet in length. Prior to the arrival of the monster wave, "this space was never filled with water...when the giant wave broke and filled it from above," reported the Strout family.

The keepers' account of this massive wall of water and its impact continued in the *Decatur Daily Republican*, with the newspaper reporting that, "Waves of ordinary size and power breaking and pressing behind added their strength to that of the monster, and the entire mass was hurled 60 feet above high water mark against the engine, boiler and foghorn house."

As is the case with many epic storms that battered Portland Head Light Station, the foghorn building did not fare well in its confrontation with the wave's violent assault. Despite its sturdiness, the force of the water wreaked havoc on the structure's brick and metal construction. In a bomb-like fashion,

the towering wave bent, twisted and shattered the foghorn building, and in the process, "the receding wave carried with it everything on shore, including stones weighing tons."

The Strout family were not the only people to recount Portland Head Light's dreadful encounter with the "monster" on the night of December 28, 1887. The *Decatur Daily Republican* captured the comments of a farmer who lived on the shore of Cape Elizabeth, some two miles beyond the lighthouse. According to the farmer, "When the wave was coming in, it made a fearful roar, but when it struck the cliffs, it seemed as though it fairly smashed them to pieces. The force of the blow was tremendous. Another such gigantic blow would have done woeful damage along the shore."

This chapter courtesy of Robert Trapani, Jr.

CHAPTER 6

LONGFELLOW

oshua Strout is the keeper who most often met with Henry Wadsworth Longfellow, America's most popular poet of the 19th century, on his many visits to Portland Head. In fact, Strout and Longfellow became close friends.

Henry Wadsworth Longfellow was born in Portland, Maine in 1807, the son of Stephen Longfellow, a Portland lawyer and congressman. His mother, Zilpah, was the daughter of General Peleg Wadsworth, a descendant of John Alden who arrived in America onboard the *Mayflower*.

Longfellow attended college in Bowdoin, Maine and one of his classmates was Nathaniel Hawthorne. He traveled the world, spent time with Alfred Tennyson and was even invited to tea with Queen Victoria. His works such as "The Ride of Paul Revere" have been memorized by schoolchildren for generations. His "Song of Hiawatha" sold tens of thousands of copies in his lifetime and "The Courtship of Miles Standish" sold 10,000 copies on its first day, which is amazing for that time in 1858. But in lighthouse circles, he is known for his poem "The Lighthouse."

In 1997, John Strout, Jr. wrote in *Lighthouse Digest* magazine about the memories as told to him from one generation of the Strouts to another about Longfellow's visits to Portland Head Light.

"Longfellow would sit with Joshua, and both would chat and sip cool drinks prepared by my great grandmother.

"Once or twice a week, Mr. Longfellow took his long walks from Portland and would bask in the sunshine of his favorite rock on the south side of the tower. He found the lighthouse reservation most enjoyable and I would like to believe he acquired at least some of his inspiration here."

At the time Longfellow visited the lighthouse area, it was but a virgin forest. Juniper bushes, alder swamps and spruces surrounded the path that led into the lighthouse reservation.

As a young newspaper reporter, Robert T. Sterling visited with keeper

Henry Wadsworth Longfellow (1807-1882)

Portland, Me. Portland Head Light.

THE LIGHTHOUSE LIFTS
ITS MASSIVE MASONRY

A PILLAR OF FIRE BY
NIGHT, OF CLOUD BY DAY

Vintage postcard of Portland Head Light, with image of Henry Wadsworth Longfellow and a line from his poem "The Lighthouse."

Joshua Strout to interview him about his memories of Longfellow. Neither Strout nor Sterling could have imagined at the time that many years later, Robert Sterling would assume the role that Strout made so famous as the keeper of Portland Head Light. Sterling timed his visits well to record those memories, as Strout died a few weeks later.

Sterling wrote: "As told to me by the keeper, Mr. Longfellow, when coming on his daily visits to the station, just bowed as a salute and then, looking up at the lighthouse, began to scan the ocean and its shores. Captain Strout never bothered the poet with questions but answered many while Mr. Longfellow was seeking information, which led up to his wonderful inspiration.

"He generally visited the lighthouse reservation after dinner each day and his long walk from the Longfellow home in Portland he termed 'his constitutional.' It was while at Portland Head that he received the color and inspiration for his famous poem 'The Wreck of the Hesperus.' But this poem was not finished until his visit to the Eastern Point Lighthouse in Gloucester, Massachusetts, where he found better established surroundings, such as 'the reef of Norman's Woe!'

"His poem 'The Lighthouse' was thought out and turned over many times while visiting Portland Head and paragraph after paragraph was jotted down on his pad of paper while at the station. It was while visiting the lighthouse reservation in the early spring, when the snow had begun to melt rapidly under the strength of the sun, that he saw the muddy water coming from the fields, swamps and emptying into the ocean that he was inspired to write:

> *I am the wave of life,*
> *and to the sea I run,*
> *To wash from me the slime,*
> *from the muddy fields of time.*

Today, there is a commemorative plaque at the lighthouse that honors Longfellow's visits to the lighthouse. Inscribed on the plaque is the final verse of his poem "The Lighthouse."

The Lighthouse
By Henry Wadsworth Longfellow

The rocky ledge runs far into the sea,
And on its outer point, some miles away,
The lighthouse lifts its massive masonry,
A pillar of fire by night, of cloud by day.

Even at this distance I can see the tides,
Upheaving, break unheard along its base,
A speechless wrath, that rises and subsides
In the white tip and tremor of the face.

And as the evening darkens, lo! how bright,
Through the deep purple of the twilight air,
Beams forth the sudden radiance of its light,
With strange, unearthly splendor in the glare!

No one alone: from each projecting cape
And perilous reef along the ocean's verge,
Starts into life a dim, gigantic shape,
Holding its lantern o'er the restless surge.

Like the great giant Christopher it stands
Upon the brink of the tempestuous wave,
Wading far out among the rocks and sands,
The night o'er taken mariner to save.

And the great ships sail outward and return
Bending and bowing o'er the billowy swells,
And ever joyful, as they see it burn
They wave their silent welcome and farewells.

They come forth from the darkness, and their sails
Gleam for a moment only in the blaze,
And eager faces, as the light unveils
Gaze at the tower, and vanish while they gaze.

The mariner remembers when a child,
On his first voyage, he saw it fade and sink
And when returning from adventures wild,
He saw it rise again o'er ocean's brink.

Steadfast, serene, immovable, the same,
Year after year, through all the silent night
Burns on forevermore that quenchless flame,
Shines on that inextinguishable light!

It sees the ocean to its bosum clasp
The rocks and sea-sand with the kiss of peace:
It sees the wild winds lift it in their grasp,
And hold it up, and shake it like a fleece.

The startled waves leap over it; the storm
Smites it with all the scourges of the rain,
And steadily against its solid form
press the great shoulders of the hurricane.

The sea-bird wheeling 'round it, with the din
Of wings and winds and solitary cries,
Blinded and maddened by the light within,
Dashes himself against the glare, and dies.

A new Prometheus, chained upon the rock,
Still grasping in his hand the fire of love,
It does not hear the cry, nor heed the shock,
But hails the mariner with words of love.

"Sail on!" it says: "sail on, ye stately ships!
And with your floating bridge the ocean span;
Be mine to guard this light from all eclipse.
Be yours to bring man nearer unto man.

CHAPTER 7

THE WRECK

One of the most notable wrecks at Portland Head Light occurred when the *Annie C. Maguire* hit the rocks on Christmas Eve in 1886. Over the years, the memories of the incident have varied but according to the Strout family's written memories, the family had just settled down at the table for a dinner in preparation to feast on eight chicken pies, which as Joseph Strout recalled were "eight of the best pies you ever tasted." Suddenly, a shout came out from his father: "All hands out! Ship ashore on the rocks!"

It was snowing and the seas were pounding fairly heavy at the time when the captain tried with all his knowledge to keep the ship from hitting the rocks, but it was too late and the timbers of the 34-year-old ship ground into the ledge by the lighthouse. Worried that the ship could break apart at any moment, the crew of the lighthouse rescued the crew of the ship, all 18 of them, including the captain, the captain's wife and their 12-year-old son, who were all able to make it safely to the shore.

Keeper Joseph Strout recalled, "We sure had a full house...I never saw such a hungry tribe in all my life. We offered them hot coffee and fed them everything we had cooked. Lucky for those men, they came on a holiday and we had an extra supply of food cooked. Once they got that chicken pie into them, the whole gang wanted to stay. They loafed around for three days while my Dad tried to convince them we were a lighthouse and not a lifesaving station."

It was John A. Strout, the third generation Strout to serve at Portland Head Light, who painted the famous memorial on the rocks in memory of the wreck of the *Annie C. Maguire* on Christmas Eve 1886. John painted the legend on his 21st birthday, the day he officially became an assistant keeper at Portland Head Light under his father Joseph. Using a boatswain's sling, he had to chip off much of the rock to make a flat surface, then make a mix of paint. Tens of thousands of tourists who visit the lighthouse view this memorial. Although it has been repainted and the words have slightly changed, the memorial was started by a Strout.

This is the actual lamp that was used to light the lens in the lantern room on the night of the wreck of the *Annie C. Maguire*. It is now in the personal collection of the Strout family.

Vintage postcard of the wreck of the *Annie C. Maguire* at Portland Head Light. This postcard incorrectly states that the lighthouse is in Portland, Maine, when in fact the lighthouse is actually located in the town of Cape Elizabeth.

The wreck of the *Annie C. Maguire* at Portland Head Light as photographed the day after the wreck. Anything of value that could be removed from the ship was auctioned off to pay debts. On the following New Year's Day after the Christmas Eve wreck, heavy swells smashed the vessel to pieces and its remains were washed out to sea as well as scattered along the coast to be picked up by souvenir hunters.

The original memorial of the wreck of the *Annie C. Maguire* was painted and placed by John A. Strout on the rocks where the wreck occurred.

Over the years, as the paint has worn off, the memory of the wreck has been repainted on the rocks. Although the wording has slightly changed and even the name of the ship is spelled differently, the wreck was immortalized by the original work of John A. Strout, a third generation lighthouse keeper at Portland Head.

CHAPTER 8

FORT WILLIAMS

obert T. Sterling wrote in 1938: "There have been many changes around Portland Head during the century and a half. A forest of spruces, fir and junipers is now cleared land. Little did Washington know or conceive at the time the lighthouse was built that there would be a great fortification surrounding it on the land side and that the great guns of war would roar so soon again."

Since 1872, when a sub-post of nearby Fort Preble was established at Portland Head Light, the lighthouse keepers and their families had to contend with a military presence.

Originally known as "The Battery at Portland Head Light," the fort became officially known as Fort Williams in 1899 — named after Brevet Major General Seth Williams, a Maine native and Civil War veteran who served as Adjutant General of the United States Army. From that time on, the fort continued to grow and expand. During World War II, it served as part of the defense to the most heavily guarded harbor in North America.

Families at Portland Head Light had to occasionally suffer through the ordeal of artillery practice from the fort and shells would sometimes literally fly over the top of the keeper's house and tower. Artillery practice would last about a week causing havoc at the lighthouse. During artillery practice, all the lighthouse dishware was taken down and packed away to prevent breakage. A report in the *United States Lighthouse Service Bulletin* of September 1, 1916 stated that Portland Head had suffered considerable damage in the past during gun practice having windows blown out, finish ripped off, roof torn open, etc. The most serious trouble reported to the Washington office of the Lighthouse Service was the damage to the brickwork of the three chimneys in the attic of the keeper's house. The bricks would be broken up and on one occasion one of the chimneys was broken off at the bottom.

Fort Williams was named after Maine native and Civil War veteran U.S. Army Major General Seth Williams (1822-1866), who served as the Adjutant General of the United States Army. He was among those present at Appomattox Court House on April 9, 1865, to witness the signing of the papers that brought an end to the War Between the States. He died five weeks later at the age of 44.

This old snapshot was someone's memory of visiting Fort Williams and one of the old guns once used to guard the harbor.

Keeper Strout had a dog that slept under the kitchen stove. When one of the huge guns blasted, the stove literally jumped off the floor. The dog was so terrified by the noise and vibration from the guns that it ran out of the house and disappeared, never to be seen again.

Arthur Cameron, son of John Cameron, who served first as the assistant keeper and later as the head keeper of Portland Head Light recalled, "Once during small caliber practice, a shell knocked a knob off the lower balcony of the tower. Had it been a standard projectile from the 12-inch gun, the tower would have been demolished!"

Unfortunately, by the end of 1943, all the large disappearing guns at Fort Williams were dismantled, leaving none for historical purposes for future generations.

After World War II, the importance of the fort declined and it was officially closed in June of 1962. Two years later, the town of Cape Elizabeth purchased the fort from the federal government for $200,000. Since then, the park has served host to thousands of picnics, concerts, weddings, and, of course, tourists. Sadly, with time, some historic parts of the fort were neglected and fell victim to vandalism and the elements. Fortunately, more recently, a nonprofit group has been formed to oversee the restoration, maintenance and preservation of what remains of historic Fort Williams.

The Goddard Mansion was completed in 1858 for John Goddard (1811-1870). It was built of native stone and was one of the first grand houses to be built along the Cape Elizabeth shore. Goddard was a successful businessman and was appointed colonel of the 1st Maine Regiment of the Cavalry during the Civil War. The mansion was acquired by the U.S. Army and was used for housing married enlisted men and their families stationed at Fort Williams. The basement was converted into the fort's Non-Commissioned Officers' Club.

An unidentified soldier posed for this photograph at Fort Williams. A large number of the soldiers who were stationed at Fort Williams were sent to North Africa in World War II.

This 1907 postcard shows the parade grounds at Fort Williams. The card was sent from V. W. Miller, 2nd Battalion, Coast Artillery Corps, Ft. Williams to Miss Sarah Welker in Cleveland, Ohio and was postmarked Feb. 8, 1909.

One of the large guns used to protect Portland Harbor. This gun emplacement was directly behind the lighthouse.

Battery gun emplacement at
Portland Head Light, circa 1940.

This vintage postcard shows a Dress Parade at Fort Williams. Interestingly, it shows both horse-drawn and horseless carriages.

Standing is Portland Head Lighthouse Head Keeper Joseph Strout. Seated is John Cameron who served as assistant keeper and later as head keeper at Portland Head Light after John Strout retired. One can only wonder how many conversations and chats the keepers had with the hundreds of soldiers from all over the United States who spent time at the fort.

Mary Strout (left), wife of Portland Head Lighthouse keeper Joseph Strout, is shown here in 1915 with unidentified wives of officers from Fort Williams.

CHAPTER 9

PLANS FOR A NEW KEEPER'S HOUSE

After years of problems with the old lighthouse keeper's house, plans were drawn up in 1890 for a new keeper's house at Portland Head Light.

The house eventually served as a duplex for the head keeper and his family and for the assistant keeper and his family.

When the lighthouse was turned over to the town of Cape Elizabeth, major renovations were made to house a museum on the first floor and a private apartment and museum office on the second floor.

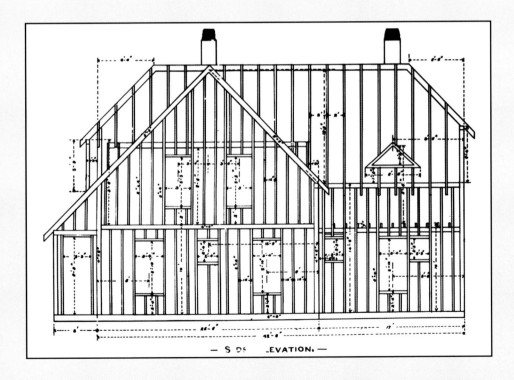

— SIDE ELEVATION. —

— FRONT. — — REAR. —

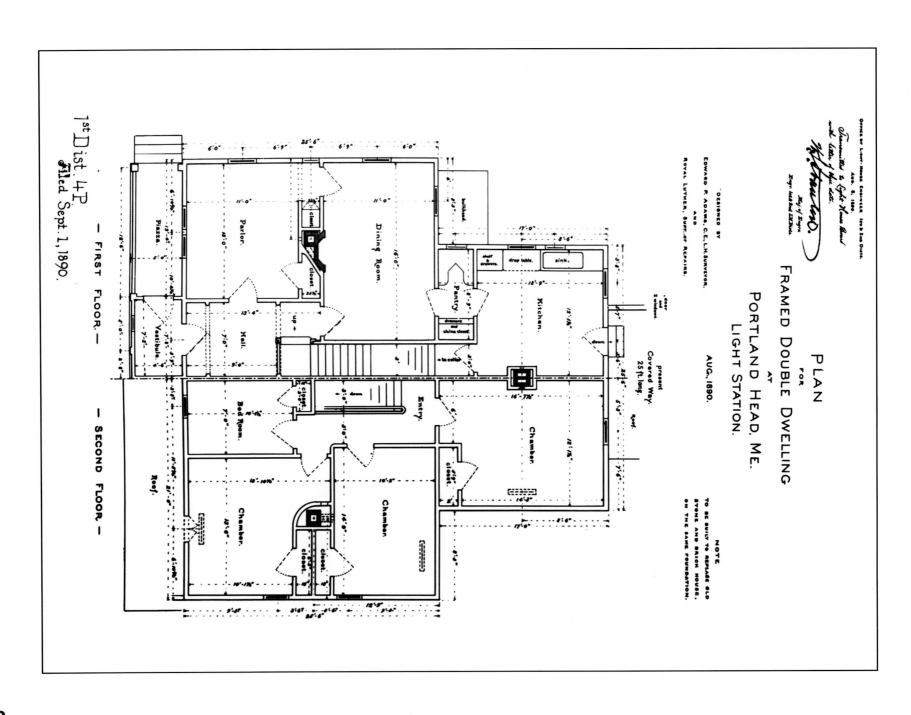

CHAPTER 10

LIGHTING THE LIGHT

John W. Cameron

After serving as the assistant keeper for a number of years, John W. Cameron assumed the position of Head Keeper at Portland Head Light in 1928, when Joseph W. Strout retired, thus ending the legacy of the Strout family that had had endured for three generations.

As a youngster in his hometown of Southport, Maine, where he was born in 1859, John Cameron had dreamed of being in the shoe business, something he did as soon as he was old enough. However, as time went on, he had a craving for the sea and served on one of the many boats he had watched as a child. He then entered the United States Lighthouse Service as a seaman on the Lighthouse Tender *Lilac* where he served under Captain Johnson.

He remained a seaman for few years when the position of Third Assistant Keeper at Cape Elizabeth's Two Lights became available. He applied for the job and was soon back on land learning the lighthouse business. Before long, he was promoted and transferred to nearby Spring Point Ledge Lighthouse where he served for two years before being transferred again, this time to serve as the assistant under Joseph W. Strout at Portland Head Light.

Having served under Joseph Strout as his assistant for over two decades, he had great respect for Joseph Strout and the Strout family of keepers. In fact, it was often said that the personalities of Joseph Strout and John Cameron were nearly identical. Both were well liked, highly respected and their genial dispositions remained the same with the thousands who shook their hands. Perhaps that is why Cameron was able to stay on as Strout's assistant for so long and why he was the natural replacement when Joseph Strout retired at the mandatory age of 70.

Portland Head lighthouse keeper John W. Cameron. He retired from the United States Lighthouse Service in 1929.

The stairs leading to the lantern room at Portland Head Light.

In 1978, John Cameron's son recalled some of his memories for an article in *Downeast* magazine and wrote:

"As a teenager, I lived through the transition of Portland Head Light from kerosene to electricity. It was a welcome change, for it relieved the keepers of the chore of 'lighting up' each night. Keeper Strout had shown me how it was done when I was a small boy. Trudging up the winding circular staircase in the light tower, we stopped on the first landing, where Keeper Strout picked up a pole about six feet long with a hook on one end. We next proceeded to the upper deck where the huge light was located. Special lenses enclosed it except for an opening in the back, which allowed for us to enter inside. Between the floor of the deck and the dome overhead were long steel-ribbed windows covered on the inside with yellow curtains to protect the lenses from the sun.

"Keeper Strout instructed me that my job was to take down these curtains by means of the hooked pole and to fold them carefully. On the way down the tower, I was to place them in a cabinet on the first deck so that they would be handy to hang up again in the morning after the light had been extinguished.

"The lamp which illuminated the light was much like any kerosene house lamp except much larger. It had three wicks arranged in concentric circles. The trick was to light these wicks with a very small flame then gradually raise it to the right height for bright illumination without causing a 'smoke-up.' If the wicks were properly lighted, they would hold a steady glow."

A popular question asked of Keeper Cameron by the tourists was how he liked the wintertime at Portland Head Light. They wanted to know how he made himself comfortable and endured the harsh winter weather at the lighthouse. His answer was always the same: "Nobody living in New England during severe winters can brag about keeping warm."

CHAPTER 11

KEEPING THE TRADITION

With the mandatory retirement of John W. Cameron in 1929, Frank O. Hilt was appointed the head keeper at Portland Head Light.

Hilt continued the tradition started by the Strouts by being a visitor-friendly keeper who wanted to share the stories of life at this famous landmark. However, Hilt had a slight advantage in gaining popularity with the advent of a popular Boston radio program on WEEL. His regular letters to the station about life as a lighthouse keeper were read on the air, and tens of thousands of people were able to learn almost firsthand about lighthouse life without ever having been to Portland Head Light. Many people, after hearing his letters read on the air, gained their first knowledge of lighthouse life, which soon led to Portland Head Light to become the most popular tourist lighthouse in the nation.

Born in St. George, Maine, Hilt started to fend for himself at the age of 13 after the death of his mother. Before long he found himself as a sailor and over time sailed on many vessels, eventually becoming the captain of the schooner *Mary Langdon* out of Rockland. After serving as the captain of several other vessels, he apparently got tired of going to sea and applied for a job with the United States Lighthouse Service.

His first position was in 1913 as an assistant keeper serving under head keeper Charles Dyer at Maine's remote Matinicus Rock Lighthouse, which is the lighthouse made famous by the heroic deeds in 1856 by Abbie Burgess, the daughter of lighthouse keeper Samuel Burgess. In 1919, when Charles Dyer transferred from Matinicus Rock to be the head keeper at Maine's Manana Island Fog Signal Station, Frank Hilt took his place as the head keeper. Although Hilt was delighted to receive the job as head keeper at the land-based Portland Head Light in 1929, he would have preferred a much quieter station farther east with less population.

Shown here on the far right is Frank Hilt who served as the keeper at Portland Head Light from 1929 to 1944. This photo was taken while he was head keeper at Maine's Matinicus Rock Light where he served from 1913 to 1929. Shown with him on the far left is 3rd Assistant Keeper Arthur Beal. The others in the middle are believed to be assistant keepers E.E. Conary and V.H. Fernald.

Assistant keeper Robert T. Sterling (l) and head keeper Frank Hilt (r) take a moment to relax at Portland Head Light. The white hats were considered to be the summer uniform hat. Sterling succeeded Hilt as head keeper in 1944 and served until his retirement in 1946. They were the last civilian keepers, left over from the United States Lighthouse Service, to serve at Portland Head Light. It was the success of Hilt's letters to radio station WEEL that were read on the air that indirectly encouraged his assistant Robert Sterling to write a book about Maine's lighthouses.

CHAPTER 12

THE LAST CIVILIAN LIGHTHOUSE SERVICE KEEPER

Born on Peaks Island, Maine in 1874, the son of a shipmaster, Robert T. Sterling started his career as a Portland newspaper reporter covering the Portland waterfront.

Although in the past he had interviewed Keeper Joshua Strout of Portland Head Light, it was while he was scooping the other newspapers with the names of the survivors of the *RMS Titanic*, which he obtained from the crew of the wireless station near Cape Elizabeth's "Two Lights," that his interest developed in becoming a lighthouse keeper. In later years he recalled that he really wanted the job as a lighthouse keeper because he felt the job would offer a great source of material to build up a stock of writing material. Shortly thereafter, he applied for a keeper's job with the United States Lighthouse Service.

Because he passed the lighthouse keepers exam with the highest score of 98% over all the other applicants, he was told he could refuse the first two appointments offered to him. Hoping to get an assignment where his wife could be with him, he immediately turned down Matinicus Rock Lighthouse feeling that the station was too remote for any kind of family life. He was then offered Halfway Rock Lighthouse, which he also turned down. He then settled on Ram Island Ledge Light, which sits on a rocky ledge in the water a short distance off Portland Head Light. Although his wife could not live there with him at this stag station, it was close to his home on Peaks Island, which would allow him to spend more time at home.

In 1915 he was transferred from Ram Island Ledge Lighthouse to Great Duck Island Lighthouse, a light station that he thoroughly wrote about in later years. From there he went on to serve at Seguin Island Lighthouse, the highest lighthouse above water in Maine and the site of Maine's only lighthouse with a gigantic first order Fresnel lens. In 1918 he was transferred to Cape Elizabeth's Two Lights lighthouse where he remained for nearly ten years before he was transferred in 1928 as the assistant keeper at Portland Head Light.

As last civilian keeper at Portland Head Light, we can only imagine what Robert T. Sterling was thinking about as he gazed out to sea. Perhaps he was reminiscing how he was able to actually live and then record the end of an era in lighthouse history, a type of history that can never again be repeated. Could he have guessed that in future years, he would be so widely remembered and admired by lighthouse historians?

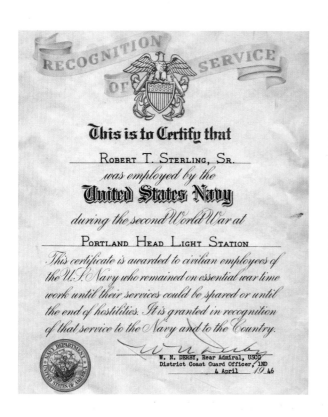

This certificate certifying Robert T. Sterling's naval service may be the most unique paper historical artifact of Portland Head Light.. This is because he was the last keeper under the United States Lighthouse Service that was dissolved in 1939 and the last civilian Coast Guard keeper at Portland Head Light. In those days, during a time of war, the Coast Guard fell under U.S. Navy jurisdiction.

In 1935, while still an assistant keeper at Portland Head Light, Sterling wrote *Lighthouses of the Maine Coast and the Men Who Keep Them*, which helped in part to record and save much of Maine's lighthouse history for future generations.

In the introduction to the book, Robert P. Tristram Coffin, a notable Maine author and friend of Sterling's, wrote: "Robert Sterling . . . at the top of his fine tower of light . . . told me about the look of the wild birds in the light of his lamp at night, about the living clouds of the spring sweeping north each March, and the ebb tide of the birds setting the other way in the fall... He is a man who has heard mystery, touched the infinite, and had his two hands deep in poetry as all light keepers have.

"Robert Sterling knows, too, what living is like when it gets down to essentials of food and shelter. What a man finds in himself when his life depends on his own two hands. What he finds when he is alone, face-to-face with himself. He knows the psychology of loneliness and the monotony of day and night. The sailors who go around the earth and see strange and fine things; but the sailors who live on the white masts that do not move, on the frozen ships that warn off the mobile from dangerous shores, though they live in a monotone that may undo some small minds, see great sights, too, and go among wide waters. For the seasons flow past them as they lie still, and the nights and days and winds and storms, never twice the same, and full of the music of eternity."

As well as writing a book and numerous newspaper stories, Robert Sterling was also interviewed by countless newspaper reporters of his time. His favorite stories to tell were about his predecessors, especially the Strout family, lighthouse keepers of Portland Head Light. One reporter after interviewing Sterling wrote: "After listening to Captain Sterling, one could not fail to have a better appreciation of the service performed by the lighthouse keepers of the Maine coast. It is such folks as Captain Sterling that has advertised Maine all over the world as the home of sturdy, resourceful men who perform their duty no matter what the cost."

Another reporter, Henry Buxton, wrote of Sterling in 1936, saying: "Captain Sterling is a salty Maine coaster from his head to his heels. Never have I met a man who smacked more of the real Maine coast with its swiftly running tides, mighty breakers smashing over sunken ledges, silver winged gulls volplaning over churning green water, salty seaweed festooned on barnacled rocks and lighthouses on isolated ledges defying frothing seas."

Upon the retirement of head keeper Frank Hilt in 1944, Robert T. Sterling rose to the rank of head keeper of Portland Head Light, a position he held until his retirement in 1946.

When President Franklin Roosevelt dissolved the United States Lighthouse Service and merged it into the Coast Guard in 1939, lighthouse keepers were given the option of joining the Coast Guard or staying on as civilian keepers. Sterling elected to stay on as a civilian keeper, thus gaining the honor of becoming the last civilian lighthouse keeper to serve at Portland Head Light. When he retired in 1946, he was one of the oldest civilian lighthouse keepers in the nation.

Robert T Sterling is shown here at the entrance to the tower at Portland Head Light during World War II. In May 1942, Lt. Thomas J. Sampson, who at that time was the officer-in-charge of the First Lighthouse and Coast Guard District, was ordered by his superiors to order the keepers at Portland Head to turn the light in the tower off as part of a wartime blackout effective on June 5 of that year. About that same time, orders also came stating that the lighthouse was to be "off-limits" to all tourists and unauthorized visitors until further notice. Sterling said at the time, "I lit the beacon for the last time and Capt. F.O. Hilt threw the switch putting it out for the last time at sunrise." Interestingly, at the same time, nearby Ram Island Ledge Light and Cape Elizabeth Lighthouse were ordered to remain lit.

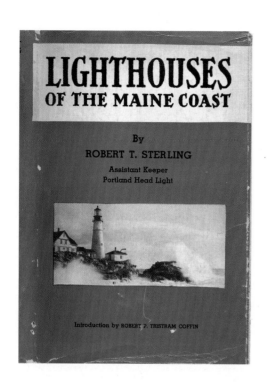

The dust jacket book cover of Robert T. Sterling's book, *Lighthouses of the Maine Coast.* Copies of the book can occasionally be found in used books stores or on Internet auction sites, but are now much more expensive than the original $1.69 selling price.

When Robert Sterling was originally asked to write his book on the lighthouses of Maine, he came up against an old ruling in the Lighthouse Service, going back to George Washington's time, which did not allow for any publicity in connection with the Lighthouse Service and its lighthouses by the lighthouse keepers. Once that ruling was overcome, the writing of his book was acclaimed by the heads of the Lighthouse Service as "remarkably accurate even to the smallest detail." In fact, Sterling's book became of vital historical significance because it gave a first-ever firsthand record of saving Maine's lighthouse history for future generations. Fortunately, Sterling was also able to continue with his writings with numerous more in-depth stories that appeared in local newspapers, which today are an invaluable source of lighthouse history.

Edward Rowe Snow was one of New England's most notable historians and authors. He wrote many books including *The Story of Minot's Light,* a copy of which he personally gave to Robert T. Sterling. When Snow presented the book to Sterling, he wrote this inscription in the inside cover. When Snow wrote his book, *Famous New England Lighthouses,* which he also gave to Sterling, he inscribed in the book when autographing it: "This particular volume I inscribe to that gifted author and his wife, Captain and Mrs. Robert Thayer Sterling. *Edward Rowe Snow.*"

Robert T. Sterling in the uniform of the United States Lighthouse Service with his dog Chang. While stationed at Portland Head Light, Sterling's wife, Martha, would often sit in her favorite chair and do her evening knitting. One evening when she went to sit down and do her knitting, Chang became irritated and started growling at the chair for no apparent reason. The dog made such a commotion about the chair that Mrs. Sterling decided to sit elsewhere. Moments later a rogue wave jumped from the sea hitting the keeper's house with such force that it smashed through the window, shattering bits of jagged glass over the chair. Had Mrs. Sterling been sitting there, she could have been severely injured or possibly killed.

Robert T. Sterling, Jr., wearing his U.S. Marine Corp uniform, is shown here with his mother, Martha Sterling, wife of lighthouse keeper Robert T. Sterling, Sr., at Portland Head Light during the mid-1940s.

Martha and Robert T. Sterling with their dog Chang during their retirement years. With the exception of Ram Island Ledge Lighthouse, Martha Sterling lived with her husband in all of the lighthouses where he was stationed.

Our favorite picture of Robert T. Sterling, the last civilian keeper at Portland Head Light, shows him at work on his manual typewriter. At the time of his death he was working on a book to be entitled The Coaster-Man, which was going to recount true experiences of Maine sea captains and seamen in the days of the great sailing vessels. Some of the memories he had planned on writing about came from Capt. Frank Hilt, another former keeper at Portland Head Light, Hilt's brother Capt. Cyrus Hilt, and Capt. Arthur Mitchell, a keeper at Maine's Fort Point Lighthouse.

Unfortunately, Sterling died before the book could be published. After his death, an unknown person, reportedly from the Bangor, Maine area, visited Sterling's widow to do a story about Capt. Sterling. Being a trustworthy person she unwittingly gave this person the folders containing Sterling's research material and photographs from his book on Maine lighthouses and partially completed manuscript from the book he had been working on at the time of his death. The material was never returned and the name of the person is unknown.

Beacons Inspire Verse
After reading Robert T. Sterling's book, *Lighthouses of the Maine Coast and the Men Who Keep Them*, J. A. Farnham of East Saugus, Massachusetts, who had summered on the Maine coast, wrote and sent this poem as a gift to Capt. Sterling.

Our Lighthouse

As I look from my chamber window at night,
Here and there on the ocean I can see a bright light;
Some shine out with quick, spiteful glare,
Others revolve slowly, as if without care,
But to a mariner's watchful eye
They spell danger or safety far and nigh.

On ledge and on reef, all covered with foam,
They guide to refuge, harbor and home.
In summer or winter, in storm and in sleet,
These faithful guardians their vigils do keep.
And when they shine out with each set of sun,
You know through the night their course will run.

Then in the morning, before the sun's bright rays,
They fade away softly smoke and haze.
All through the daylight the gray towers stand,
Like drowsy sentries guarding the land.
Again at just sunset they shine out again,
And send forth bright rays o'er the watery main.

Often I think of the men through the night,
Whose duty it is to attend to each light:
Who watch out for others from sun to sun.
God bless these men in their chosen work,
Loyal are they where others might shirk.
And when their life's voyage draws on to an end,
May they see some light to hail as a friend.

A popular photographer of the time, Ralph Blood, took this photograph of Portland Head Light showing dramatic waves smashing on the rocks. Ralph Blood and lighthouse keeper Robert Sterling both personally autographed the photograph, which is now considered an extremely valuable artifact. The original autographed photograph is now in the collection of the American Lighthouse Foundation's Museum of Lighthouse History in Wells, Maine.

CHAPTER 13

THE MIRACLE OF SUE THE DOG M.D. & D.D.S.

In the days of the lighthouse keepers, most keepers had pets or other animals of one sort or another. In fact the heroic deeds of many lighthouse dogs have been widely written about over the years. But, a couple of events in the lives of two dogs at Portland Head Light may be the most unusual of all.

Frank Hilt owned a chow named Sue that earned a reputation as a good story for any reporter, but was even more marveled upon by the veterinarians of the time.

Shown here in a rare color photograph is assistant Portland Head Light keeper Robert T. Sterling, with his dog Chang looking very happy. However, when Chang was a puppy, she was not always in the mood to be happy. It seems that Chang had a bad tooth and whenever she bit into something hard she would give out a sharp cry of pain. Sterling and even the local vet were unable to figure out which tooth was causing this problem for the poor puppy.

Then one day while the pup was gnawing on a bone, as dogs do, she let out an extra loud shriek of pain. Keeper Hilt's dog Sue was nearby and instantly ran over to Chang and immediately rolled the puppy over onto its back and held the pup down with her paws and poked her nose into Chang's mouth. While family members watched in amazement, Chang suddenly yelped in a bleating manner as Sue withdrew her snout from the pup's mouth and dropped the problem tooth onto the ground.

How a dog could pull a tooth from another dog's mouth, or even know which one to pull, is a marvel of the animal world that we humans will never know. But the facts are clear: Chang never had another tooth problem.

Another time, Chang somehow or another got a large fishhook caught in her upper lip. Keeper Hilt cut part of the hook off and then pulled the rest of it through the dog's torn lip. When Hilt's dog saw this she rushed over and,

Robert Thayer Sterling with his dog, Chang, at Portland Head Light. Both Sue and Chang were red chows and as adult animals you could not tell them apart if they were standing side by side.

just as in the previous medical emergency, rolled the pup on its back and held Chang down with her paws. She then began to lick the wound over and over and over again. Over the next week Sue continued licking Chang's wound time and time again until the torn lip was healed.

Sue, the dog of lighthouse keeper Frank O. Hilt.

CHAPTER 14

LIVING IN A FISHBOWL

ost of Wes Gamage's stories about his time as lighthouse keeper at Portland Head Light centered on tourists. His son, Dave Gamage, recalled that when his father would sometimes complain about living in a "fishbowl", he would be reminded that he basically assigned himself to the job.

Wes Gamage was officer-in-charge of the Cape Elizabeth Lifeboat Station and often served as acting group commander of the Portland Group. He was in this temporary capacity when the Portland Head Light lighthouse keeper's position needed to be filled, so he pulled a few strings and got the job.

This was not his first assignment in the Coast Guard as a lighthouse keeper. Early in his career he had temporary duty at Two Bush Island Lighthouse and later as permanent keeper at Maine's Rockland Breakwater Light from 1945 to 1950. At Rockland Breakwater, tourists were quite a challenge, especially those guests of the Samoset Resort who by virtue of Samoset advertising thought that a tour of the lighthouse was part of the their privileges.

It is important to remember that the lighthouses keeper's house, a house where the keeper and his family lived, was in fact their private home. However, because it was government property, there were many people who seemed to think that as taxpayers they could do as they pleased on government property.

Lighthouse keeper Wes Gamage's wife, Carolyn, tried hard to keep the tourists happy by actually taking down the laundry to accommodate those who were interested in taking photographs and did not want laundry hanging on the line to ruin their picture.

Weston B. Gamage, Jr. served as keeper at Portland Head Light in the early 1960s. His lobster fishing at the lighthouse provided an additional attraction for the tourists and supplemented his family's food. His son Dave recalls that he would collect all sorts of creatures from his traps and bring them back for the tourists to admire.

Dave Gamage recalled that his father and stepmother had to always keep the doors and even the first floor windows in the keeper's house locked to keep people out. They learned to be sure to always also put the ladder away immediately when they were finished using it, especially after one incident.

It seems that a particular tourist, having tried all the doors, saw the ladder propped on its side by the keeper's house and attempted to enter the keeper's house through an upstairs window. This was only unusual because it was a second floor window and it was not uncommon for people to frequently try to climb in through any one of the downstairs windows.

Dave recounted the time his stepmother was taking a bath when she heard a commotion, and then into the bathroom came several tourists with cameras in hand. She figured it was her own fault since she had forgotten to lock the door of the house.

In those days in the early 1960s, 9 am to 4 pm were the visiting hours for the park and signs were clearly posted at the gate but people never paid attention to them. Once during a Gamage family cookout in the evening, so many people came to watch them grilling that they gave it up and decided to cook indoors in the future.

Another time, Carolyn decided to sunbathe on the lawn. That did not last long either as some ladies decided they should get their lawn chairs out of the car and join her to catch some rays.

With people constantly peeking in the windows, Carolyn said she soon learned to never eat breakfast in her housecoat or curlers. She felt that most of the people were generally embarrassed as they looked in the window and saw a family gathered around the table eating since this surely was not part of their behavior that they would do in their own neighborhood.

However, Carolyn said she always felt sorry for the ladies who were looking for a bathroom. With no public facilities on the grounds, she was always willing to accommodate them, even when they did not ask nicely.

Gamage recounted to a local newspaper about one of his first assignments at the lighthouse when he became a keeper. It seems the house needed to be painted and Gamage was allotted one month to paint the entire house, inside and out. While doing the painting he often heard tourists commenting that it was a shame the government had to hire a painter while the Coast Guardsman light keeper was probably inside loafing.

As much as he thought it would have been neat to open the tower for tours on a regular basis, it would have been impossible to do, Gamage recalled. It would simply have cut into his assigned duties and he never would have gotten any work done. However, he admitted that he occasionally did open the tower for tours but generally for tour groups that had requested it by previous appointment.

Gamage recalled that one night while mowing the lawn, a couple leaned up at the fence and apologized for not obeying the visiting hour signs, but they were leaving on a plane to go home to their native New Zealand and just wanted a few minutes to take in the breathtaking view. Gamage said he gave them the full tour.

This aerial view of Portland Head Light shows the keepers' automobiles parked up close to the house. In those days there were wooden steps going down to the tide line to facilitate keeper Wes Gamage's access to his small boat that was secured off the rocks by a rope and pulley to an anchor. There was a sign at the top saying not to use the stairs, but tourists seemed to have problems reading or understanding the signs.

If you look closely at this undated vintage newswire photo, you will see the lighthouse keeper mowing the lawn and the family laundry hanging on the line.

CHAPTER 15

REMEMBERING AND HONORING

few years before his death, John Strout, great grandson of Portland Head Light keeper Joshua Strout, wrote in *Lighthouse Digest*:

"The restless computer age, in which we are trying to exist, would be incomprehensible to those of the age in which they lived. Someone once wrote that 'the Lighthouse Service is the picturesque and humanitarian work of the nation. It appeals to one's better instincts, because it is symbolic of ever-ceasing watchfulness, of steadfast endurance in every exposure and widespread helpfulness.' This puts into words the feelings of the many who have climbed the tower stairs at Portland Head Light."

While many of us who visit Portland Head Light admire its beautiful architecture and gorgeous and photogenic location, it should really be thought of as a monument to the dedicated men and women who lived here and maintained the lighthouse and kept the lights burning through every kind of imaginable weather conditions to allow for the safe travel of commerce and human life. It was through the early developement of an effective system of aids to navigation that helped build the United States into the great nation that it is today, something that was only possible through the efforts of the dedicated lighthouse keepers and their family members.

On July 4, 1952, one of Portland Head Light's former assistant keepers John A. Strout's fondest dreams came true with the completion of a two-year project to place a commemorative plaque inside the tower entryway honoring all the keepers who had served at the lighthouse since it was first established in 1791. That plaque, which had 18 names inscribed on it, included the names of his father, Joseph W. Strout, and his grandfather, Joshua F. Strout.

To get the project completed, Strout sought the help of Edward Rowe Snow, one of New England's most famous lighthouse authors and historians. Snow, who was then a director of the Massachusetts Historical League, was on hand to deliver the historical address at the time the plaque was placed. Also present was John A. Thornquist, president of the organization. Commander Christie T. Christensen, Commanding Officer of the South Portland Coast Guard Station, made the acceptance speech.

Nine members of the Strout family attended the ceremony, as did Henry Greenleaf Rogers of Yarmouth, Maine, who was the great great grandson of Portland Head Light's first keeper, Joseph K. Greenleaf.

Mem'l Tablet In Maine Unveiled By Local Man

1955

One of the principal figures at the recent dedication of a memorial tablet at Portland Head Light, Portland Me., was a Chelsea man, John A. Strout, 1 Vale st.

Mr. Strout, who holds the distinction of being the oldest living former assistant keeper at the Boston Light, instigated the Maine tablet service in honor of his grandfather and father, Joshua F. Strout and Joseph W. Strout, who were keepers at the Portland station, the first lighthouse in Maine, from 1867 to 1904 and 1904 to 1928 respectively.

The plaque honors all 18 keepers at the light since its establishment by appointment of President George Washington in 1791 when that area was part of the State of Massachusetts.

The local man unveiled the plaque during ceremonies at which Edward Rowe Snow, director of the Massachusetts Historical League, was main speaker.

Coast Guard personnel at the dedication of the Portland Head plaque. At left, I. C. Wilson, Chief Machinist, Daniel Farnsworth BMC, Douglas Mahler EN2, William Miles DC1, David Mullen S, George Ferry SN, (unidentified), and Horace Weischet ET3.

Portland Head Plaque Commemorates Keepers

PORTLAND—At a ceremony held recently at Portland Head Light a plaque commemorating all the past keepers at Portland Head was installed in the ready room. The plaque was jointly sponsored by the Massachusetts Historical League, the Bostonian Society, and the Strout family, three of whom were keepers at Portland Head.

Present were Edward Rowe Snow of Marshfield, a director of the Mass. Historical League, and John A. Thornquist, president of the organization.

About 50 people, many of them members of the Strout family, witnessed the presentation. Present was Henry Greenleaf Rogers of Yarmouth, a great-great-grandson of the first keeper at Portland Head. Rogers has a copy of the commission which George Washington gave to his ancestor establishing the light. Portland Head was the first lighthouse built in Maine.

Nine members of the Strout family attended the ceremony. Three generations of Strouts were keepers at Portland Head and one female member of the family was born and married there.

The plaque names the 18 former keepers of the light and it is installed in the ready room at the base of the tower.

Coast Guard personnel pose with members of the dedication party. Three generations of Strouts were keepers at Portland Head, and one female member of the family was born and married there. The plaque was presented jointly by the Bostonian Society, the Mass. Historical Society, and the Strout family.

This faded old newspaper clipping shows some of those in attendance at the plaque ceremony dedication honoring the keepers who served at Portland Head Light.

Old newspaper image of plaque placed at Portland Head Light in 1952.

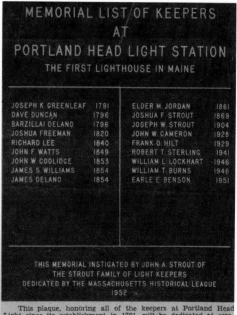

MEMORIAL LIST OF KEEPERS AT PORTLAND HEAD LIGHT STATION

THE FIRST LIGHTHOUSE IN MAINE

JOSEPH K. GREENLEAF	1791	ELDER M. JORDAN	1861
DAVE DUNCAN	1796	JOSHUA F. STROUT	1869
BARZILLAI DELANO	1796	JOSEPH W. STROUT	1904
JOSHUA FREEMAN	1820	JOHN W. CAMERON	1928
RICHARD LEE	1840	FRANK O. HILT	1929
JOHN F. WATTS	1849	ROBERT T. STERLING	1941
JOHN W. COOLIDGE	1853	WILLIAM L. LOCKHART	1946
JAMES S. WILLIAMS	1854	WILLIAM T. BURNS	1946
JAMES DELANO	1854	EARLE E BENSON	1951

THIS MEMORIAL INSTIGATED BY JOHN A. STROUT OF THE STROUT FAMILY OF LIGHT KEEPERS DEDICATED BY THE MASSACHUSETTS HISTORICAL LEAGUE 1952

This plaque, honoring all of the keepers at Portland Head Light since its establishment in 1791, will be dedicated at ceremonies in the station at 2 p. m. today. Edward Rowe Snow, director of the Massachusetts Historical League's activities, will deliver the historical address. Comdr. Christie T. Christiansen, commanding officer of the South Portland Coast Guard Depot, will make the acceptance speech.

CHAPTER 16

A MODERN KEEPER

ost true lighthouse historians will agree that the end of lighthouse keeping came to a close in 1939 when the U.S. Lighthouse Service was dissolved and merged into the Coast Guard. However, right up and into the latter part of the 1900s, our nation still had a number of keepers, although automation was also drawing that era to a fast close.

Tom and Geraldine Reed had the opportunity to be among the nation's last lighthouse keepers when Tom enlisted in the Coast Guard in 1966. After boot camp and serving onboard a 40-footer assigned to search and rescue, he was asked if he would mind helping out at Portland Head Light during the day. He was eventually offered the job of Assistant Keeper, which he readily accepted.

The Reeds have many fond memories of living at Portland Head Light; in fact their first child was born while they were stationed there during a late violent winter storm on March 24, 1967. Even though the lighthouse was on a peninsula, the access road was impassible on many occasions, and having five feet of snow was not unusual.

During the tourist season they never knew when a busload of tourists would arrive and peek in their windows, trample their flowers and ask to use the bathroom.

In 1993, Geraldine Reed wrote in *Lighthouse Digest*, the magazine of lighthouses, of her memories of living at Portland Head Light. "*Although our house was never our home, the experience of living in a fishbowl was one I cherished. Every storm brought its unique excitement. My husband spent 12-hour watches around the clock to take weather readings and maintain the foghorn and light of our lighthouse and three other lighthouses as well. When Christmas came, Edward Rowe Snow, 'The Flying Santa,' would bring us gifts by helicopter. He would check to ascertain the sexes and ages of all the members of the keeper's family and then provide very personal gifts to all. It certainly was an extraordinary experience.*"

Geraldine and Tom Reed posed for this photograph in 1993 at Lighthouse Depot in Wells, Maine. Tom served as an assistant keeper at Portland Head Light from 1966 to 1968.

THE LAST ONE OUT LEFT THE LIGHT ON

Petty Officer Davis Simpson of the United States Coast Guard and his family were the last people to live at Portland Head Lighthouse in the position of a lighthouse keeper.

Since everything was automated during Simpson's tour of duty, he was not the same type of lighthouse keeper that served at the lighthouse in the days of yesteryear. However, his responsibilities were the same as the old-time keepers and he also experienced many of the same problems with visitors as some of his modern predecessors did.

Portland Head Lighthouse was one of the last lighthouses in the country to be officially staffed, and as the media exploited that fact, more and more tourists began showing up at Portland Head to meet the last of the keepers. Simpson shared the end of the era with machinery technician Nathan Wasserstrom, also of the Coast Guard, who lived in the other half of the duplex house, and served as the assistant keeper.

Although at times it was an idyllic existence, living at one of the nation's most popular tourist attraction lighthouses had its drawbacks. For example, when the grounds were open to the public, his children could not even play in their own yard. Daughter Olivia had to ride her bike in the nearby park or at a friend's house in town.

Simpson recalled that he was constantly asked questions and many of the same questions were asked hundreds of times. Sometimes he would be mowing the lawn and would have to stop and turn the lawn mower off to answer questions. But he said he never really minded it and never had a disdain for the constant barrage of the same questions over and over.

Petty Officer Davis Simpson, the very last keeper at Portland Head Light, along with his daughters Maria (L) and Olivia (R) and family friend Rosie Williams. Photo by Bill Kalis from the August 29, 1988 issue of *Army Times*, courtesy of the *Army Times*.

The modern rotating DCB-224 that now shines from Portland Head Light gives a flashing white light every four seconds. On display in the museum you will find the original and quite valuable Fresnel lens that was originally used in the tower.

In an interview with Simpson and Wasserstrom by the *Army Times* newspaper in 1988, assistant keeper Wasserstrom recalled that a sense of humor helped, especially with one frequently asked question: "Does the foghorn ever get to you?" Wasserstrom would cup his hand to an ear, lean toward the questioner, and respond, "Huh? What?" He said he did that all the time to the tourists.

On the day the lighthouse was turned over to the town of Cape Elizabeth, Simpson was on hand to lower the colors for the Coast Guard for the last time. But he left the light on, a light that will continue to be a savior for the mariners for decades to come, thanks to the ongoing care of the beacon by the United States Coast Guard.

Entryway to the tower.

CHAPTER 18

ENTER A NEW ERA

On August 7, 1989, exactly 200 years to the day of the creation of the United States Lighthouse Service on August 7, 1789, a quadruple ceremony was held at Portland Head Light:

- The 200th anniversary of the federalization of our nation's lighthouses

- The removal of the last keepers at Portland Head Light

- The unveiling of new lighthouse postage stamps (none of which included Portland Head Light)

- The turning over of the light station to the town of Cape Elizabeth, although the Coast Guard maintained control of the tower and the light

For the big event, the government went all out with displays, dignitaries, a flotilla of ships offshore including Coast Guard vessels and even the Lightship Nantucket, and special tents were available for lunch to invited guests and other VIPs.

However, certain government officials created a public relations blunder when inviting the guests. As one newspaper article stated at the time, "It was a final salute to the men and women who have kept the light at Portland Head burning for 198 years." Unfortunately, the former lighthouse keepers of Portland Head Light were not invited.

A couple of years later, largely through the efforts of Maine's Senator George Mitchell, the actual ownership of the lighthouse was transferred to the Town of Cape Elizabeth.

The United States Coast Guard lowering the colors for the last time at Portland Head Light on August 7, 1989.

The program for the 200th anniversary of the U.S. Lighthouse Service held at Portland Head Light on August 7, 1989.

United States Senator George Mitchell and Rear Admiral Richard C Rybacki, USCG, Commander of the First Coast Guard District, at the lease signing ceremony of Portland Head Light to the Town of Cape Elizabeth on the 200th anniversary of the founding of the Lighthouse Service on August 7, 1989.

Congressman and former Maine Governor Joseph Brennan addresses the crowd at the 200th anniversary celebration of the U. S. Lighthouse Service at Portland Head Light on August 7, 1989.

The first in a series of United States lighthouse postage stamps were unveiled at the transfer of ownership and 200th Anniversary Ceremony at Portland Head Light.

A Coast Guard vessel and the Lightship Nantucket in the waters off Portland Head Light at the 200th anniversary celebration and lease transfer of Portland Head Light. If you look closely you can see Ram Island Ledge Light in the distance.

CHAPTER 19

THE MUSEUM

After a lot of hard work and major restoration and remodeling, the ribbon was officially cut and the doors of the newly remodeled former keeper's house were opened as the Museum at Portland Head Light by its first director on July 13, 1992.

On hand for the ribbon cutting ceremony was Mrs. Ethel Cameron, whose husband was born at nearby Cape Elizabeth Light and had spent his childhood growing up at Portland Head Light where his father John Cameron was keeper.

The opening of the museum was the culmination of a lot of hard work and planning by many people under the guidance of Cheryl Parker (known as Cheryl Milligan at that time), the first person to assume the position of Director of the Museum at Portland Head Light.

Also on hand for the grand opening was Frank Perdue, founder of Perdue Chicken, who was there as a guest of Gus Barber of Barber Foods in Portland.

That first summer saw lots of people who were able to view the new museum and purchase souvenirs in the gift shop housed in the former garage for the first time.

But the big event was yet to come. The actual dedication of the new Museum at Portland Head Light attended by hundreds of locals, tourists, media and dignitaries was held on September 20, 1992.

At that time, the second floor of the old keeper's house had been converted to office space and an apartment which the town of Cape Elizabeth rented. As time went on, that space eventually turned into additional space for management and inventory needed to run what has now turned into a successful and profitable gift shop and museum.

The art of maintaining and recruiting staff of mostly volunteers earned Cheryl the Governor's Award for Excellence in Volunteer Management. After being at the helm for ten years, Cheryl, now Cheryl Parker Petros, had to move on to a new life far away from lighthouses in Tennessee. In

THE MUSEUM AT PORTLAND HEAD LIGHT

DEDICATION

September 20, 1992

The Dedication program for the September 20, 1992 event honoring the newly opened Museum at Portland Head Light.

In the early stages of restoration of the keeper's house, Cheryl Parker (right) explains the plans for the design of the museum to Kathleen Finnegan of *Lighthouse Digest*.

Preparing the interior of the keeper's house for the new museum in 1992.

leaving she recalled the early beginnings of the gift shop when the money was held in a box and every sale was manually written down, and finally to the state of the art computer system which was eventually installed to track sales and inventory.

Today the Museum at Portland Head Light is under the leadership of its second director, Cape Elizabeth resident, Jeanne Gross, where she and her staff greet several hundreds of thousands of visitors a year.

The crowds gather to hear the events dedicating the Museum at Portland Head Light on September 20, 1992.

There are a number of artifacts on display in the Museum at Portland Head Light. Shown here are the U.S. Lighthouse Service hat worn by Robert T. Sterling, the last civilian keeper to serve at Portland Head Light, a brass dust pan and some dinnerware showing the last emblem of the U.S. Lighthouse Service.

The Dedication Ceremony of the new museum on September 20, 1992.

Taking a moment to pose for a photograph with the museum's first director, Cheryl Parker, at the Dedication Ceremony of The Museum at Portland Head Light, is "Mr. Lighthouse," Ken Black, founder of the Shore Village Museum in Rockland, which is now the Maine Lighthouse Museum. The Maine Lighthouse Museum has the largest collection of lighthouse lenses and machinery in a museum in the United States.

The keeper's house looks quite different in this 1990 picture with its brown bare wood when it was being renovated and restored. During restoration a porthole window that had been covered up years earlier by the Coast Guard was rediscovered.

CHAPTER 20

CIVILIAN TENANTS

Have you ever dreamed of living at a lighthouse? Well, Edward Ellis and his wife Elaine Amass Ellis did. They did not live at just any lighthouse, they were lucky enough to live at the most widely known lighthouse in the world at one of prettiest spots on the Maine coast - Portland Head Light.

After Portland Head Light was turned over to the town of Cape Elizabeth, the keeper's house was renovated and restored. The downstairs was made into a museum and the upstairs was divided into office space for the museum and an apartment. For a number of obvious reasons, the thought at the time was it would be a good idea to have someone living on the site.

In an article written in *Lighthouse Digest* magazine in 1995, Edward Ellis wrote:

> We moved in on June 6, 1993. The tree swallows were already in residence in birdhouses on the perimeter of the lighthouse grounds. The birds swirled above the movers as they carried our household possessions around the very curious tourists. Elaine and I kept explaining to visitors that the lighthouse tower could not be reached through the house.
>
> The million plus visitors to the park and lighthouse each year turned out to be only a minor inconvenience to us. The park gate is closed and locked at nightfall, which caused us to get an occasional visitor who rang our doorbell after dark when they discovered that they have been locked in. We would call the Cape Elizabeth Police to handle the release of those trapped tourists.
>
> Every March the tree swallows return. They are our faithful messengers, bringing the yearly reminder that winter really is almost over. We will watch the birds from the kitchen window as they compete for nesting space, and we will see in our minds those long, lingering summer sunsets, warm evenings, and the Scotia Prince ferry from Nova Scotia slip past the lighthouse on its way into or out of Portland's harbor. The birds will nest again in the boxes provided for them and fill our summer with their iridescent blue

Elaine Amass and her husband Edward Ellis celebrating Christmas in the 2nd floor apartment at Portland Head Light in 1995. Wow, what a place to spend Christmas!

Elaine Amass and her husband Edward Ellis enjoying breakfast in the 2nd floor apartment kitchen at Portland Head Light in 1995.

swirling and diving. They will raise another generation in the all too brief Maine summer. By mid-July they will leave their nests, and by mid-August they will be gone just as suddenly as they arrived. It always takes the human visitors longer to leave for the season; they disappear in late December.

The apartment above the keeper's house at Portland Head Light is no longer rented out. It is now used as office space and storage for the museum and gift shop.

Edward Ellis and his wife Elaine Amass in the living room of the upstairs apartment at Portland Head Light in 1995.

CHAPTER 21

POSTCARDS

H s any postcard collector is quick to point out, Portland Head Light has appeared on more postcards than any other lighthouse.

Since the introduction of postcards in America, Portland Head Light has been used to promote the state of Maine to the world, which helped in the early success of creating the state's tourism industry.

Because of its close proximity to the City of Portland, and the fact that the lighthouse stands guard over Portland Harbor, many postcard manufacturers simply assumed that Portland Head Light was within the boundaries of Portland when in fact the lighthouse is actually located in the town of Cape Elizabeth.

Featured here are a number of vintage postcards featuring Portland Head Light. Old postcards of Portland Head Light are highly sought after collectibles by many postcard collectors and some are quite valuable.

Souvenir folder
of *PORTLAND*
Maine

Portland Headlight

PLACE
STAMP
HERE

Greetings from
MAINE

Souvenir
of
PORTLAND, ME.

Post Card
This side for the address

5255 —
Portland
Light,
Portland.

PORTLAND HEAD LIGHT, CASCO BAY, PORTLAND, MAINE, OLDEST LIGHTHOUSE ON THE COAST
FIRST KEEPER APPOINTED IN 1791 BY GEORGE WASHINGTON   1577

PORTLAND HEAD LIGHT
CAPE ELIZABETH, MAINE

Cape Elizabeth, Me., Portland Head Light and Cliffs

PORTLAND HEAD LIGHT,
PORTLAND, MAINE

CHAPTER 22

IN THE MAIL

To the shame of the United States Postal Service, this nation has issued very few postage stamps honoring our nation's lighthouses. In fact they have never issued a postage stamp honoring our country's lighthouse keepers or the old United States Lighthouse Service. Yet they have issued postage stamps honoring many other branches of the government and have issued stamps honoring cartoon characters and movie stars.

In 1981, as part of its "From Sea to Shining Sea" series, the post office issued an 18-cent coil stamp featuring Portland Head Light. And in 2003, Portland Head Light was featured on the "Greetings from Maine" stamp.

In 2003, the U. S. Postal Service issued a series of postage stamps honoring all 50 states. The Maine stamp featured a moose and an image of Portland Head Light. In an effort to attract collectors, the Postal Service also sold a collectible that included the Maine state stamp and the new state's quarter which features Maine's Pemaquid Point Lighthouse on it. This was the first time in United States history that a lighthouse had appeared on American money.

This company tried to capitalize on the slogan of the stamp series by featuring North Head Light in Washington State on First Day of Issue of the Portland Head Light postage stamp.

Amazingly, this First Day of Issue cancellation of the 18-cent Portland Head Light postage stamp did not feature Portland Head Light on the color cachet cover. The manufacturer, Fleetwood, which is one of the nation's largest producers of first day covers, instead featured Maine's popular Pemaquid Point Lighthouse.

LEGENDARY MAINE LIGHTHOUSES
OFFICIAL COIN FIRST DAY COVER

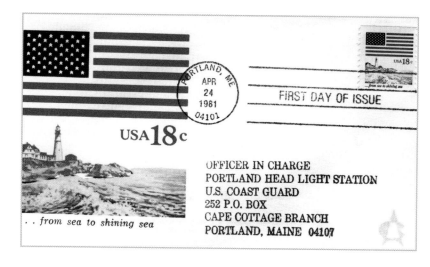

USA **18**c

OFFICER IN CHARGE
PORTLAND HEAD LIGHT STATION
U.S. COAST GUARD
252 P.O. BOX
CAPE COTTAGE BRANCH
PORTLAND, MAINE 04107

. . from sea to shining sea

FIRST DAY OF ISSUE

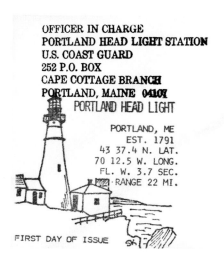

OFFICER IN CHARGE
PORTLAND HEAD LIGHT STATION
U.S. COAST GUARD
252 P.O. BOX
CAPE COTTAGE BRANCH
PORTLAND, MAINE 04107

PORTLAND HEAD LIGHT

PORTLAND, ME
EST. 1791
43 37.4 N. LAT.
70 12.5 W. LONG.
FL. W. 3.7 SEC.
RANGE 22 MI.

FIRST DAY OF ISSUE

First Day
of Issue

PORTLAND HEAD LIGHT
COLONIAL LIGHTHOUSE AUTHORIZED BY
GEORGE WASHINGTON

150TH ANNIVERSARY

PINE TREE
STATE

Maine
Statehood

1820-1970

Art Craft

PORTLAND, ME
JUL
9
1970

FIRST DAY OF ISSUE

In 1970 the post office honored the 150th anniversary of Maine statehood with a postage stamp featuring an image of Cape Elizabeth Lighthouse from a painting by Edward Hopper. The cachet cover by one of our nation's foremost manufacturers of First Day Covers featured Portland Head Light instead of the nearby Cape Elizabeth Light that was depicted on the actual postage stamp. This may have been the result of some complaints among stamp collectors and others at the time that Portland Head Light should have been featured on the Maine statehood postage stamp.

CHAPTER 23

SEA SERPENT

D o sea serpents really exist? Over the years, there have been many reports of various types of sea serpents in the waters off the Maine coast.

The May 27, 1818 issue of *The Union-United States Gazette and True American for the Country* reported one such incident in the waters near Portland Head Light.

It seems that the captain and crew of a vessel out of Castine, Maine spotted what they referred to as a "long beast" in the water, about four miles out from Portland Head Light. The creature was spotted about 1,100 to 1,200 feet from the vessel.

When asked if it could have been a whale, the captain said, "Absolutely not!" The captain said he watched the creature for at least 50 minutes, and at one time the creature raised itself about 30 to 50 feet out of the water. However, because of the distance of the creature from the vessel, none of the people onboard the vessel who also witnessed the sea creature were able to give an exact description. They lost sight of the creature when it started moving in the direction toward the lighthouse.

Arthur Cameron wrote in 1978 in *Downeast* magazine about another sea serpent. "We did have our own sea serpent off the light one morning. Devilfish, coal black and shiny with writhing arms and a head as big as a barrel, was sighted in the small bay to the south. Keeper Strout grabbed his shotgun and fired load after load of buckshot at the creature. He failed to hit it, however, for the devilfish would duck under the surface of the water as soon as it saw the gun flash."

CHAPTER 24

STAYING FIT

nyone who has a home along the ocean will tell you that oceanfront property needs special care. The old structures at Portland Head Light are exposed to all the elements that the ocean can throw at it. Maintaining the historical integrity of the property requires special care.

Over the years, Portland Head Light has had various types of repairs, restoration and renovations and of course ongoing maintenance. In 1900 the tower received major repairs when some of the stones were replaced and set in new mortar. Unfortunately, photographs of the 1900 repairs seem to have disappeared into the dusty pages of time.

Keeper Strout white-washes the tower.

Portland Head Light's restoration in 2005.

Portland Head Light is shown here after the tower was sandblasted in 1955. Charles Foster of Boston did the work. In those days a protective cover was not required. These images show features of the tower's construction that are normally not visible. After repairs, the tower was again painted white.

In 1990, the keeper's house and carriage house were restored.

The keeper's house at Portland Head Light getting scraped to prepare it for a new coat of paint in June of 2000.

The keeper's house at Portland Head Light gets some new shingles in October of 2000. Workers had decided to wait until the tourist season was officially over. They were surprised that even in October, thousands of people continued to visit the lighthouse even in the so-called "off-season."

In the spring of 2005 the tower and keeper's house at Portland Head Light received a major renovation. The $260,000 makeover project was funded from sales at the gift shop located on the grounds. CertaPro Painters, a firm that bills itself as the largest North American residential painting company, painted the tower and keeper's house.

CHAPTER 25

MEMORIES OF SHIRLEY MORONG

When the Coast Guard took over the Lighthouse Service, members of the crew on the lifeboat stations would be sent to a lighthouse to substitute for the keeper while he went on leave.

My husband, Clifton, asked for lighthouse duty and was chosen quite often to fill these leave periods until we finally got assigned to Race Point Lighthouse on the tip of Cape Cod on September 1, 1946. Conditions there were not the best - no electricity or plumbing, transportation only by a jeep with big tires - so Clif applied for and received a transfer in January 1947 to Two Lights in Cape Elizabeth, Maine.

Shortly after our arrival at Two Lights, the lighthouse was consolidated with the Coast Guard Station below the hill from the lighthouse, thus transferring the care of the lighthouse to the crew at the station. We were able to continue living in the former keeper's quarters next to the lighthouse tower, but Clif had to report to the station everyday.

In August of 1956 we were sent to Portland Head Light to substitute for BM1 Archie McLaughlin, one of the two keepers there who was going on a three-week leave. This being a double keeper's house, we stayed on the south side. William Burns and his wife Beatrice lived on the north side, but he was waiting for his retirement to go through, which did shortly after our arrival.

They left for their home down east and George Shutts was sent from the Coast Guard Station to stay until the next keeper arrived several days later.

Edward and Eloise Frank and two children came to Portland Head Light from Wood Island Lighthouse near Biddeford Pool. Because of their two children, they had wanted a mainland station and applied for the Portland Head Light position which they received.

I enjoyed our time at Portland Head and was sorry when it ended. I loved the sound of the foghorn even though it was very loud. On clear nights, the sound of the surf washing over the rocks would lull me to sleep.

Clif Morong and his two sons Jerry and Bobby.

The base of a new style of lighthouse called a "Texas Tower" being towed past Portland Head Light in 1956. It was built in Portland and then delivered to Massachusetts.

There was only one thing that bothered me at Portland Head light and that was the daily hours when the site was open to the public. We could not sit outside as we would be surrounded by people looking us over and sometimes asking many questions. In those days they were not allowed in the tower as had been allowed in earlier years and this was a disappointment to many of them. We were relieved when the gates were closed at 4 PM.

One day, Earle and Alice Benson, former keepers at Portland Head Light, called on us and they told us of a lot of damage done during a bad storm while they were stationed there. They showed us a mark on the kitchen wall caused by a rock being washed in by a wave that broke a window and flooded the floor of the kitchen and dining room. After that the first floor windows were boarded up when a bad storm was predicted.

William and Beatrice Burns in 1946 waiting for their retirement papers from the Coast Guard and duty at Portland Head Light.

George Shutts (left), a temporary keeper at Portland Head Light who filled in until Edward Frank arrived to take over the position, is shown with Clifton Morong who was filling in for keeper Archie McLaughlin who was on a three-week leave in August 1956.

Edward and Eloise Frank and children Stephen and Michelle transferred from Wood Island Lighthouse to Portland Head Light to replace keeper William Burns. They are shown here at Portland Head Light with the lighthouse dogs.

Archie McLaughlin, keeper at Portland Head Light in 1946.

CHAPTER 26

FROM THE DUSTY PAGES OF TIME

Although he transferred into the Coast Guard in 1939 and he was a Coast Guard keeper when he was transferred to Portland Head Light, Earle Benson was technically the the last person who had been a keeper with the United States Lighthouse Service to serve at Portland Head Light.

Previously he had served as the last keeper of the United States Lighthouse Service at Wood Island Lighthouse in Biddeford Pool, Maine. However, while he was stationed at Wood Island Lighthouse, the old Lighthouse Service was dissolved and merged into the Coast Guard. When keepers were given the option to remain on as civilian keepers or join the Coast Guard, Benson chose the Guard.

As well as serving at Wood Island Lighthouse, he also served at the Rockland Breakwater Lighthouse. He finished his career at Portland Head Light in the 1950s. Alice Benson, Earle's wife, recalled one incident when a woman walked right into the keeper's house at Portland Head Light and sat at the kitchen table. She expected to be served lunch and a cool drink; after all, they were government employees and she was a taxpayer.

Portland Head Light with the old style fog trumpet attached atop what was commonly referred to as the "Whistle House." The whistle house structure housed the generators that powered the fog trumpet.

John A. Strout witnessed President Theodore Roosevelt's "Great White Fleet: as it sailed around the world to show off America's might. Shown here is the USS *Alabama*, part of the mighty fleet.

Portland Head Light with the old keeper's house and the original foghorn building. Look closely and you will see the old trumpet protruding from the fog signal building which blasted the sound for the fog signal. These buildings were later replaced with the structures that are there today.

The *S.S. Regina* steaming past Portland Head Light in the early 1900s. Built for the Dominion Line in 1918, this was one of the early luxury liners to sail the great seas. In 1925 the White Star Line (builders of the *Titanic*) took over the Dominion Line and ownership of the ship. The *S.S. Regina* made its first visit from Liverpool, England to Portland, Maine on March 16, 1922. During World War II it became the official seat of the Dutch government in exile. By the mid-1940s it had outlived its usefulness and was sold for scrap in 1947 — a sad ending for such a historic vessel.

This old stereocard published for Schumacher Brothers Art Store in Portland shows the pyramid style bell tower, which was built after a hurricane in 1869 knocked the old bell tower over, nearly killing the keeper. The new bell tower held a 2,000-pound bell.

The old fogbell was put on display after the new fog trumpet was installed in the late 1800s.

John Strout (left), who was born at Portland Head Light and grew up to become assistant keeper at the lighthouse where his father and grandfather before him also served as keepers, is shown here on a visit with William T. Burns who served as a Coast Guard keeper at Portland Head Light from the mid-1940s to the mid-1950s.

Climbing the tower to the lantern room was a daily chore for the lighthouse keeper. Before the introduction of electricity, the keeper had to carry various types of oils and later kerosene to the lantern room every day. Cleaning the lens, the lighting apparatus and the windows was also required daily work.

William Burns had seen previous duty as a lighthouse keeper at Saddleback Ledge and Ram Island Lighthouses before being sent to Portland Head Light as a Coast Guard keeper. Burns was widely known for his wood-working models of Portland Head Light and other nautical items as well as handmade furniture. Burns never had any formal training in woodworking and learned the trade while stationed at remote lighthouse locations.

Vessels called "lighthouse tenders" were used to bring supplies and equipment to many lighthouses. The U.S. Lighthouse Service tender *Azalea* was used to bring supplies to many lighthouses along the Maine coast. The vessels would also often bring newspapers, books for a rotating library, and sometimes a schoolteacher for the keeper's children. Periodically, the tenders would also bring the Lighthouse Inspector, who brought a sense of urgency and fear to the keepers and their families. The Lighthouse Inspector would go over the light station from top to bottom to make sure the keeper and his family were keeping everything in working order and maintaining everything to government standards. A bad report could result in a future pay raise being denied, transfer or even the loss of the job. A good report was rewarded with an "Efficiency Star," a medal that could be worn by the keeper on his uniform. At a station that consistently received high grades, they were given the U.S. Lighthouse Service pennant which they would be allowed to display for a period of time.

You will note a dramatic difference in this photo from other photos of Portland Head Light. The roof is covered in green shingles, which was a common color the Coast Guard used for many years. Later on they changed shingles to red, but for many years Portland Head Light had a green roof.

This vintage card of a girl on top of a buoy off the coast of Maine was one of the most popular postcards of its time. Many tourists who visited Portland Head Light probably bought this card at one of the area stores.

Girl and Buoy on the Maine Coast.

Telephones were eventually installed at all lighthouses. However, in 1932, Lighthouse Superintendent C. E. Sherman was against installing a telephone at Portland Head Light. Apparently he thought that the government could save money for he wrote: "It is not considered absolutely necessary that a telephone be installed at Portland Head Lighthouse for the purpose of communication. Should an accident occur at that place, as in the case of shipwreck or other accidents in the vicinity of this light, the keepers could get communication to the outside by use of a phone on government reservation (referring to Fort Williams) not far away." Apparently the superintendent did not think much of the tourists either because he also wrote at the same time that if a phone was installed, it would require one full-time person just to handle all the telephone inquiries as to when the park was open, if one could climb the tower, etc.

In 1870, the HMS Monarch steamed past Portland Head Light in 1870 with the remains of George Peabody on board. Built in 1868, the HMS *Monarch* was the first seagoing turret ship and the first British ship equipped with 12-inch guns. In its time, it was the fastest battleship in the British Navy. It was sold for scrap in 1905. George Peabody was the co-founder of the wholesale dry good firm of Peabody, Riggs and Company and amassed a large fortune in his lifetime. During his lifetime he donated millions of dollars for a wide variety of causes including the Peabody Essex Museum of Salem, Massachusetts. In 1867, he was awarded the Congressional Medal of Honor. He died in England and his body was brought back to the States for burial in Danvers, Massachusetts on board the HMS *Monarch*.

Martha Sterling lived with her husband Robert T. Sterling at many Maine lighthouses, including Portland Head Light where he was the last civilian keeper.

Harold King was the last Commissioner of the United States Lighthouse Service. King was originally appointed District Lighthouse Inspector for the lower mid-Atlantic region around 1910. Upon the retirement of George R. Putnam, in 1934, King was appointed Commissioner. Although he personally campaigned and fought hard for the continuation of United States Lighthouse Service, he never really had a chance to succeed. Under the 1939 Reorganization Act, the United States Lighthouse Service was dissolved and merged into the United States Coast Guard. At that time, orders came from Washington to destroy or remove all items at lighthouses that contained the US Lighthouse Service (USLHS) emblem. Lighthouse keepers were given the option of joining the Coast Guard or remaining on as civilian keepers. The split was nearly even, with about half of them joining the Coast Guard and the other half remaining as civilian keepers. As the civilian keepers retired or died, Coast Guard personnel replaced them.

Many of the items used in the maintenance and daily operations of lighthouses were made of brass and many were originally manufactured at the Lighthouse Depot at Staten Island, New York. Shown here are a variety of cans and even a brass dustpan that were all used at Maine lighthouses. All of these items were stamped or engraved with the emblem of the United States Lighthouse Service or the letters USLHS. In early years the word lighthouse was two words — "light house." The items shown in this photograph are in the collection of James Claflin, a nautical antiques dealer. However, many of these types of items are on display at the Museum at Portland Head Light as well as at the Museum of Lighthouse History in Wells, Maine, at the Maine Lighthouse Museum in Rockland, Maine and at a number of other lighthouse museums around the nation.

Since most lighthouses were in remote areas, with doctors far distances away, the U.S. Lighthouse Service published a Medical Handbook, such as this 1915 edition, to deal with just about every type of medical emergency. This particular version was published by the United States Department of Commerce, which had jurisdiction over lighthouses at that time. This book is now on display at the Museum of Lighthouse History in Wells, Maine.

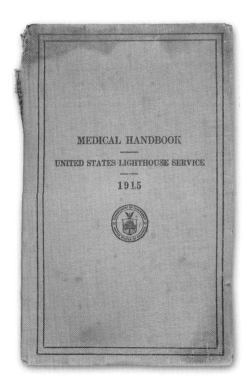

This dramatic photograph taken from the tower at Portland Head Light shows the crew of a U.S. Coast Guard 36-foot motor lifeboat rescuing fishermen of the fishing schooner *Lochinvar* on October 4, 1932. The vessel was carrying 40,000 pounds of fish and hit a submerged rock in the fog and sank.

BUREAU OF LIGHTHOUSES

U.S. Coast Guard 'hand-out' on the history of Portland Head Light for America's bicentennial in 1976.

The flag of the United States Lighthouse Service, which had been adopted in 1869, was discontinued in 1939 when the U.S. Lighthouse Service was dissolved and merged into the United States Coast Guard. Replicas of this flag are now available from Lighthouse Depot in Wells, Maine.

UNITED STATES COAST GUARD

PORTLAND HEAD LIGHT STATION

The only official government flag with a lighthouse on it today is the flag of the United States Department of Commerce. The flag came into existence in 1910 after a nationwide contest was held to come up with a design. The flag has only slightly changed since then. The motto of the Department of Commerce is "To promote the nation's economic growth" and for a number of years the U.S. Lighthouse Service operated under the Department of Commerce. The official logo for the Department of Commerce is the same as the flag that it still uses to this day. The actual flag of the Secretary of Commerce can be viewed today at the Museum of Lighthouse History in Wells, Maine.

Look closely and you will the clothes drying on the line in this photograph taken in 1900. How fresh they must have smelled from the crisp ocean breezes! As the lighthouse became more popular with the ever-growing tourism industry, future keepers' wives would find that hanging out the laundry would offend the camera-toting tourists and photographers.

CHAPTER 27

MEMORABLE IMAGES FROM THE PHOTO ALBUM

In August of 2000 representatives of the United States Coast Guard gathered with the Maine Historic Preservation Commission for a "meeting in the field" with other national members of the historic preservation community to look at federally related issues where attendees were able to see firsthand the different approaches that were taken by the United States Coast Guard to save historic properties such as lighthouses. Shown here are (L-R) John Furman, Executive Officer, CEU, USCG; Ted Dernago, Jr., Chief Real Property, CEU, USCG; Kirk Mohney, Assistant Director, and Earle Shettleworth, Jr., Director, Maine Historic Preservation Commission; and Mark Frost, Commanding Officer, CEU, USCG, Providence, and John Mauro, CEU USCG Providence.

Portland Head Light must have been a welcome sight to early mariners as it peeked through the early morning fog.

The Hood Dairy Company blimp flying past Portland Head Light. Hood Dairy was founded in 1856 and established in Derry, New Hampshire by H.P. Hood. Today it is one of the largest and most respected dairies in the United States.

Francis and Marion Porter are shown here in 1997 in the backyard of their Connecticut home with their replica of Maine's famous Portland Head Light. As a young boy Francis Porter visited the lighthouses along the Maine coast on family vacations, going even as far as West Quoddy Head Light, the easternmost lighthouse on the mainland of the United States in Lubec, Maine. But it was not until many years later when the Connecticut native, on a visit to Lighthouse Depot in Wells, decided to build his own replica of Portland Head Light so he could always have his own part of the Maine coast at home.

Have you heard of the old story about a boat being built in a basement? Well, that is what happened to Porter. Laughing as he recalled the experience he said, "We couldn't get it up the stairs and the roof had to be removed."

Porter's family helped with a lot of the work but he credited his wife Marion with making sure all the details were exact, including the flowers.

Black and white photography is often moremagnificent than color, as is shown in this close-up view of the upper part of Portland Head Light.

A cruise ship sails past Portland Head Light into the harbor. Unfortunately, many of the passengers will only see the lighthouse from the ship as they spend their free time touring Portland's "Old Port" area.

The Cunard Line's majestic *Queen Elizabeth II* steams past Portland Head Light for its first ever visit to the city in 1996. If you look closely you will see the people lined up along the shore to witness the ship's visit.

This image from a vintage postcard shows the keeper's house with a green-shingled roof during a time the station was still staffed by Coast Guard personnel. Look closely and you will notice that the flag is flying at half-staff. Also, some repairs were being done at the tower. There is a rope tied to the lantern room with some workmen at the base of the tower preparing to hoist something up to one of the outside walkways.

The U.S. Coast Guard cutter *Dallas* (WHEC 716) sailing past Portland Head Light in Sept. 2000. *Dallas* was named after Secretary of the Treasury Alexander J. Dallas, who served under President James Madison. This is the sixth cutter to bear the name *Dallas*.

CHAPTER 28

THE MANY VIEWS OF PORTLAND HEAD LIGHT

Because of the many different areas from where a photograph can be taken, Portland Head Light is one of those lighthouses that you can take hundreds of photos and each one will have its own unique appearance.

CHAPTER 29

WINTERTIME

Most of the people who visit Portland Head Light will never visit in the winter months and experience the beauty of a fresh snowfall at the lighthouse.

While looking at a wintertime photo of Portland Head Light with the bright blue sky, some will see the beauty of the location, but most will never know these are the coldest of days at the lighthouse.

While looking at a photo of Portland Head Light on a bleak, dreary and gray day, some might think they would never want to be there in the winter months, but you can be assured there is nothing more special than the solace of a lighthouse in the winter.

Although the setting is the same, each winter photograph of Portland Head Light is very unique and special.

The wintertime winds off the ocean at Portland Head Light can be bitter and bone-chilling, but there is something special about the lighthouse in those cold months that cannot be described in words or even through photographs.

CHAPTER 30

PORTLAND HEAD LIGHT
IN ADVERTISING

It would be safe to assume, and a fair guess, that more firms have used an image of Portland Head Light to promote products and services than any other lighthouse in the world.

On occasion, some of these firms apparently thought that the majesty and beauty of Portland Head Light needed to be slightly altered or changed to suit their needs to help sell their product or services.

114

CHAPTER 31

THE GHOST

Whether you believe in ghosts or not, nearly every lighthouse in America has a ghost story or two associated with it. And why not? Let's face it, every old building, with its creaking and groaning sounds, especially under the cover of darkness, can sometimes be spooky.

Let your mind drift back in time and imagine what it must have been like for a light keeper and his family at some lonely outpost along the shores or at some remote island. Hardly a day goes by that you do not have wind along the ocean and the wind can howl and swirl even more so around a light station, creating a variety of strange noises. And the human mind can often play strange tricks on you especially if you start to let your imagination get hold of you.

Some say there are no such things as ghosts. And some lighthouse historians will even go as far as saying we should never combine ghost stories with lighthouses; instead we should concentrate on telling the history of a lighthouse. To that, I say, hogwash. Whether one believes in ghosts or not, every lighthouse should have a good ghost story or two. After all, everybody loves a good ghost story.

Civilian tenants Edward and Elaine Ellis, who lived in the upstairs apartment in the keeper's at Portland Head Light in 1993 after the keeper's house was renovated, recalled in a story in *Lighthouse Digest* magazine: *"Visitors have from time to time asked us whether there are any ghosts. There seems to be a persistent belief in a connection between lighthouses and ghosts... it seems unlikely that any ghosts are in residence. However, neither of us is willing to declare that it just can't be possible. I placed a motion sensor on the stairs to our apartment in case we ever forgot to lock the door and someone wandered in. There have been times when the sensor has gone off even though no one is on the stairs. This only happens in the evening or at night. It may just be the vagaries of electronics but when the alarm goes off, we do look down the stairs and wonder."*

Geraldine Reed, who lived at Portland Head Light with her husband Tom, who was the assistant keeper there in 1962, wrote in *Lighthouse Digest* in 1993: *"One of the many peculiarities of living in a lighthouse was that we had our own ghost in residence. Rumor has it that when the lighthouse was newly built, a keeper fell to his death from the tower's spiral staircase to the cement floor below. The only place that I feel the ghost's presence was in the basement, the oldest section of the house. My feeling was that he was a friendly ghost and just needed to be told that his keeper days were over and he could rest in peace. Many years later, when I asked the Director of the Museum if she were aware that there was a ghost in residence, she gave credence to my belief that the basement seemed to be the place where he made himself known. She related occasions when she had a very eerie feeling in that part of the house."*

Portland Head Light was described in a vintage newspaper article as a living piece of lighthouse history located in Fort Williams Park. "Few people are aware that there is also an ethereal piece of history still in residence at Portland Head Light who doesn't have a clue that he has been replaced by a computer."

Silent film star Florence Turner (1885-1946), shown here in a studio still from the movie *Dark Angels*, acted in a movie filmed at Portland Head Light. She was widely publicized as the "Vitagraph Girl".

IN THE MOVIES

Since the image of a lighthouse symbolizes strength and security as well as architectural beauty, it is obvious why out of hundreds of lighthouses, Portland Head Light, more than any other lighthouse, was and continues to be used by so many businesses to help promote their products. The same reasons that attracted the advertising companies to Portland Head Light also attracted the moviemakers.

Although assistant keeper Robert T. Sterling knew in his mind the answer, in 1936 he asked one of the producers, who were at the lighthouse to film a movie, why it was always Portland Head Light that was selected to be in the movies. He was informed it was two-fold: first because of its architecture, and secondly because the setting was the best the producer had ever seen.

In the early part of the last century, a number of movies were filmed at the lighthouse. Famous actors such as brothers John and Lionel Barrymore and actress Florence Turner appeared in movies made at the lighthouse.

Arthur Cameron recalled in 1978 that while Lionel Barrymore was playing the part of a lighthouse keeper, being a stickler for realism, he borrowed a plug of B.L. Chewing Tobacco from keeper Strout saying he would pay it back when he went into town. He never did.

Arthur Cameron also recalled when actress Florence Turner was making a movie that his father, John Cameron, was hired to play the role he filled in real life as an assistant keeper. He wrote: "Pa needed no makeup, as he had a healthy tan, but the director insisted in dressing him up to look like an old sea dog."

This publicity photo was taken by the Lubin Moving Picture Company of Philadelphia as part of a promotion for a movie they filmed at Portland Head Light. Shown here (L-R) are assistant keeper John Strout, his mother Mary Strout and her husband, head keeper Joseph Strout.

CHAPTER 33

INTERVIEW WITH AN OLD WICKIE

by Richard Clayton

"Good evening sir, I'm Roger Rector,
I write for the Herald Tribune Gazette."
"Hello. What? You say you're a director?"
Asked the old man, "Umm, have we met?"

"No sir, I write stories for a newspaper,"
Said Roger, "and I came here to see you.
You're the best by far lighthouse keeper,
And my editor wants to know what you do."

"Well, every morning I go to the lantern room,
Wind up and fasten the motor-weight of the clock,
Lower the lamp table and get out the broom,
Extinguish the lamp and clean out the flintlock.

"Wipe the chimney with tender loving care,
Then wrap it in a dry cloth to keep it dust-free,
Remove the lamp and see to its repair,
And clean the lantern glass of the salt of the sea."

"What about the shipwreck?" asked the writer,
"Didn't you row out in a storm and save a life?"
"I was supposed to do that," said the lamplighter,
"It was my duty. I rescued the ship captain's wife.

"The station's life-saving crew was in a larger boat,
And those brave lads saved the rest of the crew,
The waves were so high; it was hard to stay afloat,
And that cold northern wind chilled me clear through.

"But, I'm not in their crew, I was just helping out,
Those life-saving men man a surfboat, that's tricky,
They are professionals and know what it's about,
And if they need a little help, they call the old wickie.

"Late in the afternoon, just before the sun sets,
The fishing boats try to make port before night,
They're swabbing the decks and storing the nets,
And as the red sun is sinking, I light the light.

"You can tell your editor that this is the job I do,
I tend the light and stand watch until eight,
Then the assistants take over and I'm through,
I'm on duty before dawn, so I don't stay up late."

"How should we remember you?" asked the writer,
"When we look at the lighthouse on a dark night?"
The keeper smiled and his old eyes shone brighter,
After a pause, he slowly said, "He kept a good light."

The poem "Interview with an Old Wickie" could well have been written in memory of Captain Joseph Strout, keeper at Portland Head Light.

U.S. Lifesaving Service drill practice in the waters off Portland Head Light.

CHAPTER 34

LIGHTS WITHIN SIGHT

Ram Island Ledge Lighthouse

When looking out to sea while standing near the tower at Portland head Light, one can easily see directly in front of you Ram Island Ledge Lighthouse. Completed in January 1905, the first keeper to live there was William C. Tapley.

This was the first station where Robert T. Sterling, who later went on to become keeper at Portland Head Light, was stationed. A local newspaper reporter, Henry Buxton, who for many years was well acquainted with Sterling, referring to desolate Ram Island Ledge Light wrote in 1936: *"Captain Sterling served an apprenticeship in solitude — He came into contact with all phases of the life of a lighthouse keeper, the problems of fog and winter gales when monster seas boiled over sharktooth ledges and roared in demonical fury against the very foundation of the station, threatening to engulf and dash the occupants into eternity."*

A later keeper, Joe Johnson, who lived there in the mid-1900s, described life as isolated, like living in the 1800s, but also said he was never really lonely. One winter, he and another keeper spent over a month and a half stranded at the lighthouse, with their last week of food being oatmeal three times a day.

In 1959 the last keepers were removed and the lighthouse was automated and today its light is run by solar power. The lighthouse is now licensed to the American Lighthouse Foundation, a nonprofit national lighthouse preservation organization that is headquartered in Maine.

Inside stairway at Ram Island Ledge Light.

In 1905, William Converse Tapley became the first lighthouse keeper at Ram Island Ledge Lighthouse. He was no stranger to lighthouse living, having been previously stationed at Maine's Saddleback Ledge Lighthouse from 1890 to 1896 and Deer Island Thorofare Lighthouse from 1896 to 1905. He then spent the next 14 years living on this lonely desolate rock until his retirement in 1929.

Close-up view of the lantern room area of Ram Island Ledge Light.

Spring Point Ledge Light

From Portland Head Light, looking northeast toward Portland you will see the Spring Point Ledge Lighthouse at the end of a long breakwater. This lighthouse, referred to as a "spark plug" style lighthouse because of its shape, was built in 1897 and was once totally surrounded by water. The last keeper was removed from the lighthouse in the mid 1930s. In 1951, the 900-foot long breakwater was built to the structure, which is now owned by the Spring Point Ledge Light Trust and managed by the Portland Harbor Museum. From time to time the museum opens the lighthouse for public tours.

Vintage postcard showing Spring Point Ledge Light surrounded by water before the breakwater was built to it. Note that the boat used by the keeper to get back and forth to the lighthouse.

Vintage postcard showing both lighthouses at Cape Elizabeth Two Lights.

Entering the U.S. Lighthouse Service in 1869, Frank Lewis Cotton later served as head keeper at Cape Elizabeth Lighthouse.

Two Lights at Cape Elizabeth

About eight miles southeast of Portland Head Light, one can see the twin lights of Cape Elizabeth, known more commonly as "Two Lights." Established in 1827, they were the first twin lighthouses built on the Maine coast. They were built as range lights — meaning sailors would line them up to know they were on course into Portland Harbor. The original towers were eventually torn down and replaced in 1874 by the towers standing there today. The west tower was eventually discontinued and sold to the highest bidder in 1959 and is still in private ownership today. The keeper's house next to the east tower has been privately owned for years. Tens of thousands of tourists who visit Portland Head Light will also go to view and photograph Cape Elizabeth's Two Lights; however, if you do so, please remember the lighthouses are surrounded by private homeowners and please respect their privacy. The east tower, which is still an active aid to navigation, is now licensed to the American Lighthouse Foundation but is not open to the public. To learn more about the American Lighthouse Foundation and their Museum of Lighthouse History in Wells, Maine, go to their website at www.LighthouseFoundation.org.

When the large second order lens from the East Tower of Cape Elizabeth Lighthouse was removed, it was put on display in the Cape Elizabeth Town Hall where it remains to this day.

Vintage postcard showing the Cape Elizabeth Two Lights as well as the old Life Saving Station and Radio Beacon Station at Cape Elizabeth. The large two-story building in the center is now used as housing for Coast Guard personnel.

This view of Two Lights is from the days when many of Maine's lighthouses were painted chocolate brown or red. This was done to make them stand out better as daymarks in snowstorms.

Whether these people are family members of the keeper or guests visiting the lighthouse are unknown, as is the year of the photo. However, you will see by the pole that telephone lines had been brought to the lighthouse by this time. The area looks quite different today.

When the west tower of Cape Elizabeth's Two Lights was discontinued, it was sold at auction and has been privately owned for many years.

This early photograph of Cape Elizabeth Two Lights clearly shows the surrounding landscape before the area was built up.

Vintage postcard of the original Cape Elizabeth Life Saving Station at Dyers Cove that was built in 1887. The U.S. Life Saving Service was considered a sister organization of the U.S. Lighthouse Service and was established for the sole purpose of rescuing people from shipwrecks. Dedicated to their cause, their motto was "You have to go out, but you don't have to come back." The end of the Life Saving Service came in 1915, when the U.S. Life Saving Service and the U.S. Revenue Cutter Service were merged to form the new United States Coast Guard. When a new station was built in 1933, the original Life Saving Service Station was sold and moved away.

The east tower and keeper's house of the Cape Elizabeth Lighthouse as it appears today.

Although Halfway Rock Lighthouse appears to look in good condition in this photograph, the interior of the tower is in poor condition. In 2004, Maine Preservation listed it as one of the ten most endangered historic properties in Maine. The light in the tower is now lit by the solar power from the panels shown here. Halfway Rock Lighthouse is now licensed to the American Lighthouse Foundation, a nonprofit lighthouse preservation group based in Wells, Maine.

Halfway Rock Lighthouse

On a clear, sunny afternoon, you will be able to see Halfway Rock Lighthouse 10 miles out in Casco Bay. Built in 1871, the lighthouse was automated in 1975. Lawrence E. Johnson, Jr., who died at age 53 in 1996, was one of the last lighthouse keepers stationed there. His father recalled after his death that his son was assigned to the station for three-week stints; however, rough seas often changed that because relief keepers were unable to land. In fact when his enlistment in the Coast Guard was over, he was forced to remain at the lighthouse until the weather changed, allowing for safe departure.

The lighthouse, which is now licensed to the American Lighthouse Foundation, can most easily be seen from Land's End on Bailey Island, Maine. Listed by Maine Preservation as one the ten most endangered historic properties in the state, efforts are underway to raise money for its restoration.

As night falls at Halfway Rock Lighthouse, the beam shines brightly.

The modern optic now in Halfway Rock Lighthouse is no comparison to the original Fresnel lens that was once in the tower.

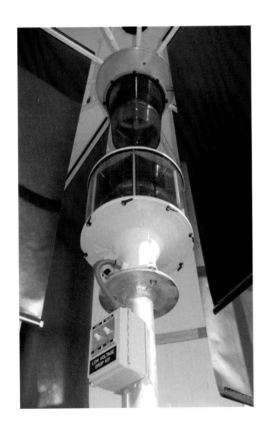

Vintage postcard of Halfway Rock Lighthouse. The fog bell tower to the right tower to the right is no longer standing.

CHAPTER 35

NOT SEEN FROM PORTLAND HEAD, BUT NEARBY

Situated in "Bug Light Park," dedicated to the people who built the Liberty Ships at this location during World War II, is the Portland Breakwater Lighthouse, known locally as "Bug Light." The tower that stands here today is the second lighthouse at this location. The current tower was modeled after the Greek Choragic Monument of Lysicrates in Athens, Greece. After being dark for many years, the lighthouse was re-lighted on August 14, 2002.

The original Portland Breakwater Lighthouse was a short wooden tower that was first lit on August 1, 1855. With no keeper's house at the site, during violent weather the keepers literally had to crawl on their hands and knees over the narrow breakwater wall to reach the lighthouse.

In 1875, the first Portland Breakwater Lighthouse was removed from the site to nearby Little Diamond Buoy Depot. As shown below, its lantern room was removed and a watch room was installed so it could be used as an observatory. Suffering from neglect and beyond repair, it was eventually demolished.

Portland, Me. Breakwater Light.

The second and final light at Portland Breakwater was established in 1875. However, it was not until 1889 that a keeper's house was added. Prior to that, the keeper lived nearby and had to walk along the breakwater to the lighthouse to maintain it. The size of the keeper's house was expanded in 1903. This vintage post card view of Portland Breakwater Lighthouse shows a six-masted vessel in the harbor. This card, and the one on the opposite page, mistakenly place the lighthouse in Portland in its caption, when in fact it is actually in the community of South Portland, Maine.

William T. Holbrook, a Civil War veteran, devoted most of his life to service in the United States Lighthouse Service. He served as a keeper at Halfway Rock Light, (1885-1890), and other Maine lighthouses including Bass Harbor (1890-1894) and Burnt Island Light in Boothbay Harbor (1894-1909). He finished his career at the Portland Breakwater Lighthouse, the location where his wife died. After he retired, he was very active in a variety of civic groups in and around Portland.

Breakwater Light, Portland, Me.

Vintage postcard of Portland Breakwater Lighthouse showing the station from the water.

This photograph of the Portland Breakwater Lighthouse was taken in 1894. The lighthouse was automated in 1935 and discontinued in 1942, and the house was demolished. Only the tower remains today. Over time, the inner side of the breakwater area was filled in with land.

CHAPTER 36

IT LOOKS LIKE A LIGHTHOUSE

Towering high above the Portland skyline is the famous Portland Observatory. When tourists and visitors first see it, many of them think that it is a lighthouse.

But nothing could be further from the truth. It is the only surviving signal tower on the east coast of the United States. Built by ship owners in 1807, it used a system of signal flags to indicate which incoming ships were planning to dock hours before they arrived. This allowed the dockworkers to prepare for the ships' arrival, notify the ships' owners that the vessels had arrived safely, and also to let the crew's loved ones know that they would soon be home.

The structure was built by selling shares that were all eventually purchased by Capt. Lemuel Moody, giving him full ownership of the tower. Capt. Moody received a fee from over 100 ship owners to display their signal flags. Upon Lemuel's death in 1846, his son Enoch operated the tower until his death in 1870.

It was Capt. Lemuel Moody, with the use of his telescope from the top of the Portland Observatory, who gave the people of Portland a running account of the famous sea battle between the USS *Enterprise* and the HMS *Boxer* during the War of 1812. After the American crew of the *Enterprise* captured the *Boxer*, it was Capt. Moody who notified the people of Portland that he saw the flag of the United States flying from the captured British warship.

When over one-third of Portland was destroyed in a fire in 1866, the Observatory was one of the city's survivors. With the advent of radio when many of the observatories around the country met the fate of the wrecking ball, the Observatory again survived. In 1939 it was taken over by the city and declared a historic site. It almost met its fate again in 1995 when it was discovered that beetles had infested the wood of the tower. However, preservationists came to its rescue and the tower was saved. In season it is now open to the public and one can climb the tower with its spectacular view of Portland Harbor.

Vintage postcard image of the Portland Observatory

The Portland Observatory recently underwent major restoration to bring it back to pristine condition.

Vintage postcard of the Portland Observatory.

The Portland Observatory appears as though it is standing guard over the City of Portland. The Portland Observatory is open Memorial Day to Columbus Day from 10 am to 5 pm daily. The last tour departs at 4:40 pm. There is a small admission fee. If you cannot climb the Observatory, you can go on the Internet to www.portlandlandmarks.org where you can see breathtaking views from the top of the Observatory updated every two minutes.

CHAPTER 37

I WISH I WERE A LIGHTHOUSE

By Gerry Braun

I wish I were a lighthouse,
Shining oh so bright,
My beacon would help everyone,
Throughout each and every night.

I would never be lonely,
As I look upon the sea,
There are ships everywhere.
Wherever my light might be.

Some say I'm no longer needed,
That my age is catching up to me,
But I feel just as important,
As I could ever be.

Look, I've got a new coat of paint!
My stairs repaired and strong,
I'm now again open for visitors,
But will I be that way for long?

But since I'm not a lighthouse.
And I will never be,
I hope that all lighthouses,
Will be safe for history!

IN CLOSING

Portland Head Light's last civilian lighthouse keeper, Robert T. Sterling, is shown here with his dog, Chang, returning from an evening walk, or perhaps from a visit with some of the soldiers at the fort.

Sterling served as the assistant keeper at Portland Head Light from 1928 to 1943 and as head keeper from 1943 to May of 1946.

Because this is a color photograph, it is considered to be of great historical importance. It also shows the keeper's house with a charcoal gray roof and gray trim.

It is quite possible that this photograph was taken on Robert T. Sterling's last day as the keeper of Portland Head Light.

ABOUT THE AUTHOR

Tim Harrison of Wells, Maine is co-founder of Lighthouse Depot, editor and co-founder of *Lighthouse Digest* magazine, co-author of five lighthouse books and president of the nonprofit American Lighthouse Foundation.

In 2004 Harrison retired from the day-to-day activities of Lighthouse Depot to enable him to devote more time to *Lighthouse Digest* magazine and the American Lighthouse Foundation.

As editor and publisher of *Lighthouse Digest* magazine, Harrison, along with his partner Kathleen Finnegan, has led its development from a newspaper print publication to a high-quality glossy magazine that now has subscribers in all 50 states and 17 countries.

Harrison co-founded and has served as president since 1994 of the American Lighthouse Foundation, a nonprofit, national, all-volunteer preservation group that has helped save lighthouses all around the nation. The group now has 22 lighthouses under its auspices, 11 of which are in Maine which it is restoring or maintaining, including the tower at Pemaquid Point, which under his leadership became the first land-based lighthouse in Maine to be opened to the public on a regular basis. Under Harrison's leadership, the American Lighthouse Foundation has been able to establish alliances and working relationships with the United States Coast Guard and local community leaders in establishing chapters of the American Lighthouse Foundation to assist in saving lighthouses.

Under Harrison's leadership, the American Lighthouse Foundation became the first nonprofit in all of New England to obtain ownership of a Maine lighthouse under the National Historic Lighthouse Preservation Act, which is a complicated and strict application process. In 2001, after being dark for 26 years, the Little River Lighthouse in Cutler, Maine was relit as a Beacon of Freedom to the World, an event that was recorded by the History Channel and aired on national television. Little River Lighthouse, once listed as one of the ten most endangered historic properties in Maine, is now on its way to becoming fully restored.

Harrison founded the Museum of Lighthouse History which has on display some of the most rare items left in existence from the days of the U.S. Lighthouse Service. Many of the items on display were donated from his personal collection.

Harrison is an original supporter, and later, through the American Lighthouse Foundation, an original sponsor of the Great Lakes Lighthouse Festival. The festival has raised tens of thousands of dollars for various Great Lakes lighthouse restoration projects. In 2004, Harrison was honored as the first recipient of the Great Lakes Lighthouse Festival Volunteerism Award for lighthouse preservation.

Harrison has co-authored a number of lighthouse books, including the best-selling books *Lost Lighthouses* and *The Golden Age of American Lighthouses* as well as *Endangered Lighthouses*.

He is an active preservationist and has appeared in numerous radio and television interviews, including Nightline and Made in Maine. Harrison has written hundreds of articles about lighthouses and has one of the largest collections of vintage lighthouse photographs in the country. He has given hundreds of lectures on the need to save our nation's lighthouses and their history. Several years ago he completed the film *Lighthouses of Maine, A Journey Through Time*, which aired on PBS-TV.

Tim Harrison in the Museum of Lighthouse History in Wells, Maine.

In 2004, under Harrison's leadership, the American Lighthouse Foundation saved Maine's endangered Prospect Harbor Lighthouse from imminent collapse, thus saving one of the last conical wooden towers in America.

Harrison says his biggest concern now is that time is running out to locate and save the memories and photographs of the few surviving children of the lighthouse keepers who served under the United States Lighthouse Service, which was dissolved in 1939 when it was merged into the Coast Guard.

For the past six years, Harrison has been leading a campaign to honor the men and women of the United States Lighthouse Service with a series of postage stamps. It was also his idea to create a National Memorial honoring the people of the United States Lighthouse Service, something he hopes will some day become a reality.

In August of 2005, Rear Admiral David Pekoske, USCG, personally honored Harrison with the medal for Homeland Security's United States Coast Guard Meritorious Public Service Award, one of the highest awards given by the United States Government to a civilian. The award was given to Harrison for his many and varied efforts in helping save America's lighthouses and the history associated with them.

Tim Harrison is shown here with Cindy Williams, Todd Gutner, and Charlie Berg (cameraman) of WCSH-TV Channel 6 in Portland in 2005 for a first-ever, full half-hour live broadcast about the lighthouses of Maine on the evening news.

The Tower Spirits

This Historic Lighthouse was built in 1791 ~ When the first keeper was appointed by President Washington.
Wherein, thirty dedicated keepers up these eighty-nine steps did climb ~ Right up to its automation in 1989.
Yet, within this Portland Head Light Tower ~ For over one hundred years still shines their midnight hour.
Left herein these two Spirits from another time remain ~ Still trimming the wick and lighting the flame

THE PHOTOGRAPHY OF MICHAEL FRANCIS BARRY, NEW ENGLAND'S HISTORY ARTIST

Just as the poet Henry Wadsworth Longfellow was often inspired at Portland Head Light, so is internationally renowned maritime photographer Michael Francis Barry who can often be found at the famous lighthouse.

A Maine native, Michael handmade his own large format 8" x 10" camera and all his images are created by using light sensitive 8" x 10" photographic film. His work, as featured here, is often available at Portland Head Light or directly from him through his website www.MichaelFrancisBarry.com.

The Tower Spirits

According to folklore, former keepers stationed at the Portland Head Light had seen two spirits, a man and a woman, inside the tower. These spirits are said to emanate a very tranquil kind of energy: that of peace and harmony, protection and security. Many of the keepers and kin accepted these two benevolent spirits into their families as the "other" members. Specific identities and background information about these two spirits are currently unknown. However, what is known is that both spirits had been seen or heard beginning around the mid-19th century. Could this be true? Or could it be that it was just the wind and the sea which created those ghostly sounds heard inside the tower by these former keepers? Perhaps even today the tower is still settling into its centuries-old foundation. What about those believed sightings? Maybe they were just merely phantom figments imagined by an overworked and exhausted keeper. Or just possibly these two spirit keepers might still have an eternal bond to this, their beloved tower . . . and they have just simply decided never to leave.

Michael Francis Barry's prints are available in: 18" x 24" for $30 or 11" x 14" for $15, plus $5 shipping. Designed to fit into standard- sized, easy-to-find frames, all photographs shown here are signed in gold ink by the artist and attractively shipped in gold tubes and ready for gift giving. To order, visit www.MichaelFrancisBarry.com or write to Lights, P.O. Box 632, Portland, Maine 04104.

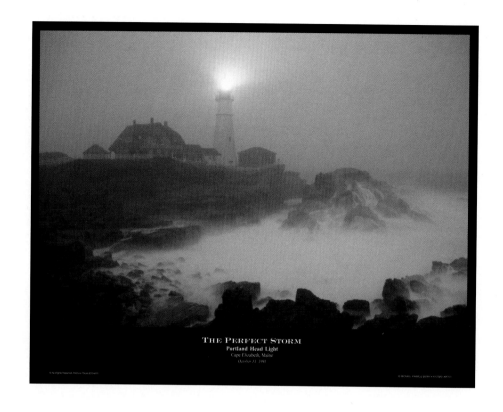

THE PERFECT STORM
Portland Head Light
Cape Elizabeth, Maine
October 31, 1991

The Perfect Storm

Two hundred years almost to the day after it went into service, Portland Head Light stood up against what has been billed "The Perfect Storm, " a storm stronger and more intense than any in recorded history. It began as Hurricane Grace on the Florida coast, but later became the "No-Name" storm as it moved towards New England colliding with a high-pressure cold front coming down from Quebec, and a low-pressure zone near Sable Island (The Graveyard of the Atlantic). It was a Halloween nightmare for everything in its path. The giant waves, hurricane winds and heavy seas smashed against the walls and windows of the great white tower. The dignified tower, once again, did not falter. This natural force of apocalyptic proportions covered an area of 1500 nautical miles, from Gloucester, Massachusetts to the Grand Banks.

"The Perfect Storm" at Portland Head Light as was captured on film by Maine artist Michael Francis Barry in the late afternoon of Halloween 1991. The artist was only able to remain on location for about 20 minutes to create this 5-minute time exposure, as the developing conditions had become extremely dangerous. The following day, the very same fence that the artist had climbed over to record this image had been washed out to sea, only to be replaced by various sized rocks strewn all across the area, where the Artist had been standing just hours before. All prints are signed in gold ink by the artist.

Michael Francis Barry's prints are available in: 18" x 24" for $30 or 11" x 14" for $15, plus $5 shipping. To order, visit www.MichaelFrancisBarry.com or write to Lights, P.O. Box 632, Portland, Maine 04104.

150

Let It Snow

No other lighthouse can symbolize the beauty of the holiday season as does Portland Head Light after a fresh and crisp Maine snowfall.

This one of a kind and unique photograph of the Portland Head Light was captured on film for the first time ever on a cold New England Winter's Night. The artist himself, Michael Francis Barry, spent several days on location personally decorating this lighthouse using 63' of garland, 9 holiday wreaths, 13 red bows, special holiday window curtains, two cut pieces of stain glass for the triangular roof windows, (green & red, to represent port & starboard), and he also added a special blue bulb for the porch light. This was a nighttime time exposure of 15 minutes as the snow storm was just moving out to sea. All prints are signed in gold ink by the artist.
Michael Francis Barry's prints are available in: 18" x 24" for $30 or 11" x 14" for $15, plus $5 shipping.

Designed to fit into standard-sized easy to find frames, all photographs shown here are signed in gold ink by the artist and attractively shipped in gold tubes and ready for gift giving. To order visit www.MichaelFrancisBarry.com or write to Lights, P.O. Box 632, Portland, Maine 04104.

PHOTO CREDITS

Cover - Craig Leist
i - Ross Tracy
1 - Lighthouse Digest archives
2 - Lighthouse Digest archives
3 - Library of Congress
4 - National Archives
5 - Lighthouse Digest archives
6 - U.S. Coast Guard
9 - Strout Family
10 - Strout Family
11 - Lighthouse Digest archives
12 - Strout Family
13 - Strout Family
14 - Strout Family
15 - Lighthouse Digest archives
16 - Lighthouse Digest archives
18 - Lighthouse Digest archives
19 - Lighthouse Digest archives
20 - Lighthouse Digest archives
21 - Lighthouse Digest archives
23 - Lighthouse Digest archives
24, top - Lighthouse Digest archives
24, bottom left - Strout Family
24, bottom right -
    Lighthouse Digest Archives
25 - Town of Cape Elizabeth
26 - Lighthouse Digest archives
27 - Lighthouse Digest archives
28, top left - Private Collection
28, top right,
    Lighthouse Digest Archives
28, bottom left - Strout Family
28, bottom right - Strout Family
28 - National Archives
30 - National Archives
31 - Cape Elizabeth Historical Society
32 - Bob Trapani, Jr.
33 - Dave Gamage
34 - Elaine Jones
35 - John Sterling
36 - John Sterling
37 - Lighthouse Digest archives

38 - John Sterling
39 - John Sterling
40 - John Sterling
41 - Lighthouse Digest archives
43 - John Sterling
44 - John Sterling
45 - Dave Gamage
47, left - U.S. Coast Guard
47, right - Lighthouse Digest archives
50 - Strout Family
51 - Lighthouse Digest archives
53 - Bill Kalis, Navy Times/
    Army Times
54 - Bob Trapani, Jr.
55 - Lighthouse Digest archives
56 - Lighthouse Digest archives
57 - Lighthouse Digest archives
60 - Lighthouse Digest archives
61 - Lighthouse Digest archives
62 - Lighthouse Digest archives
63 - Lighthouse Digest archives
64 - Lighthouse Digest archives
65-70 - Lighthouse Digest archives
71-73 - Lighthouse Digest archives
75 - Lighthouse Digest archives
77 - left, Strout Family
77 - right. Lighthouse Digest archives
78, left - Museum
    at Portland Head Light
78, right - Rusty Nelson
79 - Lighthouse Digest archives
80 - Lighthouse Digest archives
81 - Lighthouse Digest archives
82 - Lighthouse Digest archives
83 - Shirley Morong
84 - Shirley Morong
85 - Shirley Morong
87 - Lighthouse Digest archives
88 - Lighthouse Digest archives
89, top and right -
    Lighthouse Digest archives
89, bottom left - Maine Historic

Preservation Commission
90, left - Library of Congress
90, center and right - Strout Family
91 - Lighthouse Digest archives
92 - Lighthouse Digest archives
93 - Lighthouse Digest archives
94, left - John Sterling
94, center - Edith King
94, right - James Claflin
95 - John Sterling
97 - Lighthouse Digest archives
99 - Lighthouse Digest archives
100, left - Charles Crocket
100, right - Martha Earles
101, left - Lighthouse Digest archives
101 - Library of Congress
102, left - Leon Zawicki
102, right - David A Rodger, Portland
Press Herald, Maine Sunday Telegram
103, left - Lighthouse Digest archives
103, right - U.S.C.G. Historian's Office
105, left - Pam Brown
105, right - Robert Dennis
106, top left - Janine Lawther
106, bottom left - Bob Gizinski
106, right - Allan Wood
107, top left - Bob Sankey
107, top right - Linda Gochee
107, bottom left - Leona Rush
107, bottom right - Leona Rush
108, left - Leona Rush
108, right - David W. Throne
109, top left - Anne Mylecraine
109, bottom left - Karen Oakes
109, right - Karen Oakes
110 - Darrell B. Parker
111 - Bob Trapani, Jr.
112 - Dan Kehlenbach
116 - Ken Carle
118 - Lighthouse Digest archives
119 - Strout Family
122, left - Strout Family

122, right - U.S. Coast Guard
124, left - Tommy Dutton, USCG
124, center - Shook Michigan
    Lighthouse Conservancy
124, right - Tommy Dutton, USCG
125, left - Lighthouse Digest archives
125, right - Robert M. Washburn
126, top left -
    Lighthouse Digest archives
126, bottom left -
    Cape Elizabeth Historical Society
126, right - Lighthouse Digest archives
127, top left -
    Lighthouse Digest archives
127, bottom left - National Archives
127, right - Lighthouse Digest archives
128, left - Kim Turner
128, right - Lighthouse Digest archives
129, left - Lighthouse Digest archives
129, right - Susan & Ed Maciej
130, left - Tommy Dutton, USCG
130, right - Michael Francis Barry
131, left - Tommy Dutton, USCG
131, right - Lighthouse Digest archives
133, left - Joyce Abbott
133, right - U.S. Coast Guard
134, left - U.S. Coast Guard
134, right - Lighthouse Digest archives
135, left - Deborah Conley
135, right - Lighthouse Digest archives
136 - Lighthouse Digest archives
137 - Lighthouse Digest archives
138, left - Phil Bradley
138, right - Lighthouse Digest archives
139 - Lighthouse Digest archives
140 - Lighthouse Digest archives
143 - John Sterling
146 - Bob Trapani, Jr.
147 - Ann-Marie Trapani
156 - Nina Trapani

American Lighthouse Foundation
P.O. Box 889
Wells, Maine 04090
www.LighthouseFoundation.com
207-646-0245

KIDS ON THE BEAM

WE ENCOURAGE YOU TO JOIN TODAY!

Since 1994, through successful restoration projects, our museum of Lighthouse History, our quarterly publication Tower Notes, and our web site, the American Lighthouse Foundation has been leading the way in saving lighthouses. Only through your help can the American Lighthouse Foundation continue.

MUSEUM OF LIGHTHOUSE HISTORY

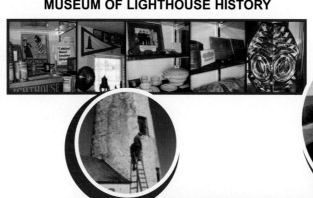

Help save America's Lighthouses!

Lighthouse DIGEST

SUBSCRIBE TODAY!

The Magazine of Lighthouses

Special Offer:
Subscribe for 1 year for $28.00 And
Lighthouse Digest
Will Donate $5 to the

American Lighthouse
Foundation

Sign me up for: ☐ **$28 for 1 Year**   ☐ **$49.50 for 2 Years**

Name: _____
Address: _____
City: _____ State: _____ Zip: _____
Email: _____

USA $28, Canada $38, Overseas $46

Saving Lighthouses, One Subscription at a Time.

Lighthouse Digest

P.O. Box 68, Wells, Maine 04090 — Call toll free 1-800-668-7737
www.FogHornPublishing.com